Jocelyn Galsworthy

WHITE HATS AND
CRICKET BATS

Sir William Becher's five favourite grounds

pastel

Jocelyn Galsworthy

WHITE HATS AND CRICKET BATS

MY PAINTING LIFE

with foreword by Henry Blofeld

SWAN·HILL
PRESS

First published in the UK in 2000
by Swan Hill Press, an imprint of Airlife Publishing Ltd

British Library Cataloguing-in-Publication Data
  A catalogue record for this book
  is available from the British Library

ISBN 1 84037 179 X

Typeset by Servis Filmsetting Ltd, Manchester
Printed in Hong Kong

Swan Hill Press

an imprint of Airlife Publishing Ltd
101 Longden Road, Shrewsbury, SY3 9EB, England
E-mail: airlife@airlifebooks.com
Website: www.airlifebooks.com

For my Mother and Tita

Acknowledgements

I owe a debt of gratitude to JAV, who knows me well, and without whose help this book would never have been written; to Pat Berry, who typed my manuscript most beautifully and who was unfailingly understanding and patient; to the marvellously tolerant and talented John Simmons for his superb photography of my original work; and (although he does not know it) to the brilliant Jack Russell for the inspiration derived from his book *Caught on Canvas*. He and I share a passion for painting cricket, but I am not nearly such a good wicket keeper!

Material has been quoted, either *verbatim* or paraphrased, from *An Alien's Fortress* by James Gindin.

All illustrations not otherwise stated are the work of Jocelyn Galsworthy.

Foreword by Henry Blofeld

*I*t gives me the greatest of pleasure to write the Foreword for this most handsome volume. It not only contains so much of Jocelyn Galsworthy's most outstanding work but it is also the first part, I hope, of an ever-growing and enchanting pictorial record of the foremost cricket grounds of the world. Her talents, as illustrated between these covers, are unique just as her presence under her white sun hat and idiosyncratic mini-umbrella, at any and every major cricketing occasion stamps it with the final seal of authenticity and approval. What she has managed with her delicate, sensitive and subtle use of pastels is remarkable even to an expert. To a layman such as myself, it is mind-boggling.

One of the main joys of this collection is that Jocelyn has not confined herself only to the Test Match grounds of the world. Some of her finest offerings are of the smaller, more out-of-the-way grounds which may never host games above the club, village or school level. There is here a wonderful cross-section and although Lord's may be Lord's, I am not at all sure that I wouldn't rather hang Hurstbourne Priors, the HAC ground in the City of London or Upper Club on my walls.

In Jocelyn's short autobiography which accompanies all these lovely pictures, she has held her pen with nothing if not a forthright grip. She plots her place as the present carrier of the flame in the long and distinguished artistic progress of her famous family and tells us how much she owes to her mother from whom she obviously inherited much of her skill. She also manages to give the present generation of England's cricketers a fierce buffet or two around the ears.

I am not certain I would go quite as far as she has in her criticism of County cricket in comparison to District cricket in Melbourne, but no doubt she has her reasons. With pen and pastel she has produced a most engaging and delightful book which will greatly enhance the bibliography of the game. It will too, invoke countless happy memories, either as player or spectator, for everyone who turns the pages. It should find a place on all our shelves.

Henry Blofeld

Preface

Galsworthy is a name which is hard to live up to; it is a name which carries in its wake an artistic and literary reputation far beyond my aspirations. To me it is an intriguing fact that when Queen Mary commissioned the furniture and *objets* for her famous Dolls' House, the works of Galsworthy, reduced to miniatures, formed part of the library along with William Shakespeare and other giants of English literature.

At the opening in 1962 of Birmingham University's Galsworthy Rooms (a collection of papers, paintings and memorabilia relating to John Galsworthy), I found myself seated next to learned professors on both sides. I felt quite out of my depth but, nevertheless, managed to steer the conversation towards cricket – a subject very dear to my heart even then.

Compared with my illustrious great uncle, my talent for painting pictures is tiny, but I share with him a capacity for the hard work and perseverance he deemed absolutely necessary to put one on the road to success. That road has, indeed, been long and steep and I leave you to judge whether I now have a shorter distance in front of me than behind.

The following pages depict my painting life in pictures and in words, a life which has not always been devoted to cricket (although the game itself has featured prominently when I was either watching my father and brother playing or accompanying them to County matches). It is my hope that the reader will derive much pleasure from my paintings and the telling of my story.

J.M.G.
1999

Contents

Limited Edition Prints

Introduction

A woman painting on the boundary, surrounded by boxes and boxes of chalks, with her grey hair streaming out from under her white cricket hat (worn to dispel the glare), could be mistaken for an eccentric. This label does not worry me a bit. For a little over fourteen years I have painted school, club, County and Test matches up and down the country and recently abroad as well, and everyone knows that I love all aspects of the game. Women who love cricket, and there are many of them, are passionately enthusiastic and very knowledgeable.

Nowadays, when I settle down to paint a match, I am greeted by the regulars and through the medium of television am now known to many members of the public. Many write to me or telephone, and we have long, animated conversations about the game. It is not just the match itself, at whatever level, which appeals to me, it is everything surrounding it: the preparation, the acquisition of the best vantage point from which to paint, the anticipation of the match itself, the spectators, the thrill when England does well, the barmy army and even, when it is all over and I am still there, the deserted ground redolent with the excitement generated only half an hour before. Afterwards, there is the getting together with like-minded friends from the cricket world, dissecting the match, discussing the talent and making plans for the next occasion.

A painting usually takes five or six days to complete and I turn up at the empty ground well before a match and long after it has finished, as I paint everything from life and, only exceptionally, from a photograph.

Painting cricket has now become a way of life which suits me very well. Having always been an outdoor person, I never mind the heat. However, in this country it is usually too cold rather than too hot and I am often swaddled in layers of jumpers when painting early in the season. This is all part and parcel of the life I have chosen for myself, and I feel infinitely fortunate to be able to devote it to a profession I love. Portrait painting can be very lonely, but depicting cricket in all its forms brings me into contact with so many marvellous people that I feel I have friends wherever I go.

Sporting art, unfortunately, attracts little praise from those who profess to know. For some reason, it is usually regarded as the poor relation of landscapes and portraits. Pastels too, are not taken as seriously by the establishment as oils. My outside paintings are always done in pastel, for very practical reasons as well as for personal preference. However, I am equally at home with oils. In my view, good quality sporting art will always be held in high esteem by those who feel it is part of their heritage, and who share a passion for cricket or any other sport. As times change and cricket evolves, I hope to be there to record it in all its forms.

Chapter 1   The Galsworthy Heritage

My parents, Yvette Johnstone-Nicol and Hubert Galsworthy, were closely related. My father's mother was my mother's great-aunt, her grandmother's sister. The two Spanish sisters from Gibraltar had married two school friends from Harrow, Alec Johnstone-Nicol and Hubert Galsworthy.

The Johnstone-Nicols in those days were extremely well off, the Galsworthys less so, but both led comfortable lives at Weyhill near Andover and Torquay respectively. My maternal great-grandfather Alec blotted his copybook in no uncertain terms when, at the age of twenty-four, he married a Catholic. He was in the Black Watch where officers were in any case not allowed to marry until they were twenty-five, and coming from a strait-laced Scottish Protestant background these two sins were not easily pardoned. He had to leave his regiment, and spent the remainder of his life (he died at forty-five) living in grand style, thus leaving his widow very little. His eldest son Billy, my grandfather, joined the Black Watch during the Great War and was severely wounded. He never really recovered, contracting tuberculosis at the end of the war and dying aged thirty-three. His

widow, my grandmother, was then faced with the task of bringing up two small daughters Yvette (my mother) and her sister Yvonne, alone and in a foreign country.

Madame Alice, as my grandmother liked to be known, was a thoroughly practical French woman from Dinan in

My maternal great-grandfather Alec Johnstone-Nicol

Great-grandmother Catalina

My maternal grandparents, Billy and Alice, living it up in Cairo

My paternal grandfather, Hubert Galsworthy

My paternal grandmother, Angelina Galsworthy

Brittany. She had a little money from Billy and supplemented it by putting her bilingual talent to good use whenever possible. As the exchange rate at that time very much favoured the pound, she was able to live quite comfortably in France for part of the year, staying with her French family in Paris. As soon as the Second World War broke out, she offered her services to the government as a censor where her French mother tongue and perfect English were a godsend. My mother Yvette also helped the war effort in the same department as she was fluent in both French and German.

As for the Galsworthy side of the family, my grandfather Hubert (the brother of the writer John Galsworthy), the most silent in public and the least intellectual of the four Galsworthy children,[1] did not have a profession. He spent the greater part of his time playing golf, for which he won endless cups, watching cricket as a member of the MCC and sailing his magnificent yacht moored on the River Dart. His son, my father Hubert, was born in 1906 and had the conventional upbringing of those days, being sent to preparatory school in Devon followed by Sherborne where he excelled at all sports, particularly rugby. He later played rugby for Hampshire. He was destined for the Royal Naval College at Dartmouth but when his eyes were examined it was found that the sight in one of them was extremely poor as a result of an

Muriel Galsworthy (Tita) with Ting-a-Ling   (Photo H.J. Galsworthy)

Grandmother Angelina   (Photo H.J. Galsworthy)

uncorrected 'lazy' eye in childhood. Today, of course, this would have been discovered and treated very early on.

It was a huge disappointment to him. Hubert and his sister Muriel (my beloved Aunt Tita, simply known as 'Tita'), lived with their Spanish mother after she had separated from my grandfather – a highly unusual move in those days. They had been incompatible for years and an amicable parting seemed the only way out. In the event, this left my grandmother with very slender means, and she was unable to lead the life to which she had become accustomed, with a large house and many servants. However, as soon as my father left Sherborne, a very happy and hospitable household was established outside Winchester, in a modest house with fifty acres given to my father at the age of eighteen by his Uncle Jack, as John Galsworthy was known.

When my grandparents separated, it was my Spanish grandmother Angelina Orfila, who attracted all the Galsworthy good will. She was well loved by her mother-in-law Blanche Bartleet Galsworthy who, realising that her son, Hubert, was too feckless to look after his children's interests, instructed Uncle Jack to see that provision was made for them. Angelina and Blanche were of one mind when it came to untidiness, mistakes in etiquette and the structure of society in general and there was a natural bond between them. When Blanche died in

1915, she left all her money to my father.

In this carefree, loving household young Yvette and Yvonne would spend their school holidays with their first cousins once removed, Hubert and Muriel, whom they adored. Yvette and her sister had been sent to a convent in Hertfordshire, and on one of their visits to the Galsworthys it was discovered that they spoke with what can only be described as a regional accent. Tita was horrified. If there was one thing which had been drilled into the Galsworthys (mainly through Blanche), it was correct pronunciation. Tita recalled that: 'When I was three, my grandmother visited and was shocked to hear me talk. "You must do something with that child", she told my mother. "She's speaking Cockney." It was the nurse and, of course, my mother, whose English was never very sensitive, simply didn't know.'[2] When the same thing happened to Yvette and Yvonne, Tita immediately informed their mother that they must not stay at that particular convent a moment longer. A school of the right sort was very quickly found for them.

Yvette was not particularly academic, and at that time not particularly pretty either, but she was immensely practical and excelled at sport, so much so that she managed to arrange a nice little barter system. She would be on this or that team in exchange for her homework being done. Yvonne, by contrast, was very clever, very

Hubert John Galsworthy, my father

Yvette Galsworthy, my mother

(Photo H.J. Galsworthy)

pretty and no good at sport. She was a wonderful actress and mimic. Yvette was the proverbial ugly duckling who later grew into a beautiful swan. Eventually, by dint of being thrown together on so many occasions, Hubert and Yvette fell in love and in 1941 were married in the Catholic cathedral in Edinburgh. My father was in the RNVR and stationed in Scotland.

It was into this somewhat unusual family that I was born in May 1942, followed in 1944 by my brother John. By this time my father had set up a thriving poultry farm on his smallholding, and judging from the diaries he kept before I was born, life had been the greatest fun. He played tennis, danced, sailed his own yacht which he kept on the Hamble, rode to hounds, shot, played bridge and was thoroughly spoilt by his mother and doting sister.

My father decided to take up photography and his work appeared regularly in the *Tatler* and *The Yachtsman* before the war. He produced some stunning studies with his wonderful eye for composition. After the war, he took it up seriously and there was hardly a family of note around Winchester who did not have their wedding and christening done by him. My mother had wanted him to concentrate on photography and distinguish himself in that field, but he lacked the will despite my mother's enthusiasm on his behalf.

At the outbreak of war my father applied to join the RNVR but was turned

'A Dragon on the Solent' photographed for The Yachtsman *by H.J. Galsworthy*

My posthumous portrait of John Galsworthy, OM   *pastel*

Jocelyn Galsworthy

Jocelyn, aged 12, harrowing the field

(Photo H.J. Galsworthy)

down at his first interview because of his eyesight. Undeterred, he was given a second interview and told the admirals that he could see better with his one eye than they could with their two! This time he was accepted and soon commanded his own minesweeper. After the war he and a fellow commanding officer published an amusing collection of rhyming verse taken from the imaginative signals sent between their minesweepers.

U₃U   V (from)   U₂U

When daily sweeping operations were completed and ships returned to anchor, some C.O.s arranged to berth together. Duty free spirits had become increasingly difficult to get and any stocks that still remained were sadly depleted.

We send our compliments to you,
And having found some gin we think
You'd better come and have a drink.
It will not be a mighty tot,
But still, the best that we have got!

So come across and join us please
In semi-Bacchic revelries!

U₂U   V   U₃U

How kind of you to ask us in
To drink your last remaining gin;
But should we then imbibe the lot,
I'll see you get what we have got.⁵

My mother, on the other hand, would not fulfil any of her ambitions until very much later in life when she determined to 'find herself'. She became an extremely talented artist.

From a very early age I was aware of my illustrious great-uncle, John Galsworthy. The other members of the family, particularly his sisters, were also highly talented. His sister Lilian was a poet in her own right and had married Georg Sauter, a German portrait painter of note. Her home became a salon until the First World War, with guests like the painter Whistler, Mark Twain, Ezra Pound and Joseph Conrad who, with his wife, became a close friend. Their son Rudolph (Rudo Sauter) was an artist, musician and poet. He became secretary of the RBA (Royal Society of British Artists) and literary agent for the John Galsworthy Estate. His other sister, Mabel, a talented pianist who had a large studio with two grand pianos in her house in Camden Hill, supported the debuts of Harriet Cohen and Myra Hess as well as Betty Humby, who later became Lady Beecham. With this background, I felt that I had no choice but to achieve some sort of distinction myself.

It soon became obvious that my talent would be for drawing rather than anything else. I had wished to be musical but since, as I discovered later, I was the only girl in the whole school who could not carry a tune, I was not going to have that particular wish granted. I started to draw any and everything, in particular tractors and farm implements. My father's smallholding a few miles outside Winchester provided a ready source of tools, implements and tractors for my attention. We had two farm helpers, Ned and Jim, who had been Aunt Tita's cubs before the war, but were now cowman and handyman respectively. I played at being Ned and my brother was Jim. By the time I was seven, I was driving a tractor and harrowing the fields, determined to make myself useful. John and I did not mix with other children very much, enjoying an idyllic childhood with our imaginations and each other for company. I then graduated to ponies and filled endless sketchbooks with my feeble efforts, but they got better and better until, by the time I went to school, unusually not until the age of ten, I was able to get a good likeness and represent most things fairly

Jocelyn and John, 'Ned and Jim'   (Photo H.J. Galsworthy)

accurately.

Tita, so called because my father when little was unable to say the word 'sister', gave me an idea of perspective. My brother used to join me for these lessons but he did not have much patience for learning at that time. In fact, Tita taught us both our lessons – French, Latin, English, history, geography and maths until we finally went to school. We had a solid grounding in drawing and the use of watercolour. We always made our own Christmas and birthday cards, and at that time my brother could draw as well as I could but was

not encouraged to think of becoming an artist.

Tita and my grandmother left the house at Winchester in 1951 as it was too small for two families. They returned to their beloved Devon and rented a house in Paignton. John and I used to live with them during term time, returning to our parents in Winchester for the holidays. It was a strange arrangement, but one which worked very well. My father was once accosted at a smart drinks party and quizzed as to why he did not have his children at home. His reply was that a grandmother's influence is very valuable in a child's early life, which is probably true but it was also highly convenient for him not to have us under his feet all the time. My Spanish grandmother was deeply religious, and my aunt equally so. This had a profound effect on me as a child, and I am glad that I was exposed to their brand of Catholicism which has stood me in good stead all my life. In their household, good manners and devotion to duty came before everything else. However, there was also much fun and laughter too, and I can honestly say that I missed nothing by not going to a conventional school at an earlier age.

We left Paignton and rented 2 Beyrout

Cottages, in Plymouth while Tita and her mother looked for a permanent house. John and I were mad about the Navy and would march up and down, down and up in our back yard, pretending to be sailors. We so desperately wanted to be a naval school that Tita (always game) called us the Beyrout Naval School and embroidered badges for our blazers and hats. We were inordinately proud of our 'uniforms'.

We always had to go for a walk after lunch, come rain or shine, and though we jibbed at this sometimes, Tita used it as an opportunity to teach us about nature. We learned to recognise birds, flowers and trees. We collected flowers and dried them, and watched for the early signs of spring. We were taught so many things for which there is no time today and I know that Tita's civilising influence meant that I became responsible and mature in outlook at an early age, and grew up in an unspoilt, if somewhat unworldly, way. I cannot speak for John since he always used to hide under the table when French lessons came round, and proved a more than reluctant scholar. One day, the education authorities called to see my aunt and grandmother to

An early effort

demand to know why John and I were not at school. My grandmother, an autocratic Spaniard, barely five feet in height, would stand no nonsense from them and saw them off. They never came back.

Life resumed its even tenor, interrupted only by excitements such as the visits of our cousins from Gibraltar. Suddenly, without warning, my grandmother suffered a massive heart attack which was all but fatal, and we then set about our house-hunting in earnest. She had to be on the flat, so we left Plymouth and

settled in Seaton, a small seaside town on the Devon coast. John and I found ourselves at the Stella Maris convent in Seaton. I settled in happily enough, but poor John (by now a complete tearaway) fell foul of the nuns at every possible turn. They despaired of him. Eventually, he went to Twyford School in preparation for Downside. I, on the other hand, was forbidden to go to boarding school by my father who thought them unsuitable for girls. I stayed at Stella Maris, moving to their senior school across the road at the age of eleven. I was in my element there, becoming head of house and head girl by the time I was thirteen. Our house always won everything (being naturally bossy I made sure of that). I loved games and was captain of hockey and tennis. I was certainly no 'goody-goody' and in fact, I think I must have been one of the naughtiest, but somehow I always avoided being caught.

At fourteen, I left the convent and went back to Winchester, where I was privately tutored for my O levels but before that, I spent six marvellous months in Spain with my aunt. My grandmother had died and it was decided I should accompany my aunt to Spain to learn Spanish. It was an experience not to be missed.

My brother, first at Twyford and then at Downside, showed a great aptitude for, and a love of, cricket which was encouraged by my father during the holidays. We had a cricket net erected in the garden with a proper wicket and I used to bowl endlessly to John. I made him practise fielding non-stop and as I myself could catch any cricket ball that came my way, I was very intolerant if anyone fielded badly. Meticulously, I arranged his holiday matches, which we played mostly at Twyford School. I was the scorer, my father and the opposing captain's father were the umpires, and my mother did the teas. These were hard-fought matches and my father kept very strict discipline. Cricket became a passion with me and remains so to this day. Little did I think that I would be so fortunate as to earn my living painting the game.

[1] James Gindin, *An Alien's Fortress* p28
[2] *Ibid* p29
[3] *PAD* or M/S *Nonsense Verses* by Lieutenant-Commander J. A. B. Harrisson DSC, RNVR and Lieutenant-Commander H. J. Galsworthy RNVR.

Chapter 2   Broadening Horizons

My first real trip away from England, was to Spain with my aunt after her mother had died. I realise now that I was a true innocent abroad, totally naive and young in some ways for my age. Everything amused me and I was easily pleased. We stayed with our cousins, the Patrons, outside Gibraltar, but we could do little to cheer up my aunt who was still feeling the loss of her mother. I remember going to a huge lunch party with all the Spanish cousins and the aristocracy of Jerez de la Frontera. My aunt sat next to a contessa who was sympathetic over my grandmother's death. 'Tell me, my dear, how long is it since your poor mother has been gone?' When Tita told her that it had been six months, she was horrified that Tita was not in mourning – that is, wearing black. My aunt wore navy blue at the request of her mother who did not like black, but this was not approved of and I am afraid to say that my aunt was very frowned on, such were the conventions in Spain in those days.

The Spaniards we met were great fun and great talkers. Maria Patron had a cook and a gardener, who like most servants then were taken very much for granted. It was heaven for me who had never known what it was like to be waited on, and while I felt for them being made to run here and there at a moment's notice on some whim of their mistress, I observed how genuinely they loved the family and especially the children. The cook had been with them for forty years and I am sure counted herself one of the family.

My aunt grew gradually happier and her natural good humour and love of life surfaced once more. She kept Maria Patron and her sisters vastly amused with her funny stories and contributed much to the general atmosphere of contentment. The entire family dutifully observed the teachings of the Catholic Church, bringing religion into their daily lives in a light-hearted way. This made a profound impression on me and to this day I believe in living as they did. It is the strength and comfort of my religion which carries me through good times and bad and which gives me peace of mind. I remember Tita going to confession, naturally in Spanish, which she spoke tolerably well, though what such a truly good person could have had to confess is beyond me. As with all languages, certain expressions, literally translated, do not always have the intended meaning or more often than not, no meaning at all. I well remember the priest laughing fit to burst at something my aunt had said. She never revealed what it was, no matter how hard we pressed her.

Life at this age was wonderful. I passed the time painting, lunching, sight-seeing and laughing. I mixed with people older than myself most of the time, which did not matter to me, but must have coloured my views on life. I never rebelled as a teenager, nor even felt the need to behave in a way which might upset my family. This, I gather, is unusual but the sense of duty which seems to have been bred in me precluded such behaviour. It may also have led later to a difficult choice between family and career.

Every week our wonderful cousins from Gibraltar, Laurie Vasquez and her daughter Eva, would take us out to the mountains for the day in their car. We had a marvellous time, screeching loudly as we negotiated the perilous hairpin bends on rocky partly unmade roads, stopping at beauty spots for a tasty picnic, or lunching in some little restaurant by the roadside. I was desperately sad to have to come home in August 1957. It was a terrible wrench and I felt very homesick for Spain where I had been wrapped in the security of a close-knit family. I do not think I have ever been as happy as I was then.

It was here in Spain that I started painting in oils, first doing a picture of the house in Puente Mayorga. It had a truly Spanish view from the terrace of tiled roofs and olive trees with the mountains beyond. Tita also painted some water-colours at the same time and was always very critical of my drawing which she helped me correct. This was the start of my painting from life outside. My aunt would never have allowed me to draw from photographs as is so prevalent today, or even use them for reference.

As well as painting, I had promised to

Self-portrait 1959,   *oil on canvas*
Signed 'Jocelyn' in the manner of Rembrandt-
a phase I went through at the time

apply myself to Spanish lessons, and the headmaster of the local school was roped in to teach me. My mother had written to me reproving me for, apparently, playing rather than working, so a more stringent timetable was put in place and I was left in no doubt that I had to learn Spanish before returning to England. I progressed fairly well and under the eye of my aunt (who was as much a stickler for good Spanish as good English) I became quite proficient. Later on, in addition to my O Level Spanish, French, English and Latin, I was to take A Level art at Winchester College of Art as well as a secretarial course 'just in case' as my father used to say. It was my wonderful mother more than anybody who put me on the road to painting, as she was determined I was going to be an artist.

In 1957 my mother took John and me to Brittany. My maternal grandmother had come from Dinan originally, and I have found the Brittany coast the greatest inspiration ever since this first holiday. St Malo is a fascinating old town, reputedly a pirate stronghold with a tide which goes out six miles, providing spectacular scenery which I have painted constantly over the years. The first of these efforts

was on this initial visit. I sat on the wall above the Plage du Mole while John and my mother went fishing. I was left there to paint. They returned two hours later to find me in tears because I could not get it right. My mother told me not to worry but to try again the next day. This time the painting progressed much better. It took three days to finish and was not bad for a first attempt. I painted the beach, the

ramparts and the people on the beach who continue to be as colourful today as they were then. On my return, I exhibited this painting at the Winchester Art Society.

My mother had rented a small villa from a French couple, enthusiastic Communists, who had decamped to a hut in the garden to make room for us. When some respectable English friends came to stay, they were scandalised by the attitude of *Monsieur* as well as by his drunken behaviour. But, to us, who took a more liberal view, the couple were a constant source of amusement. My sheltered upbringing had not prepared me for the earthier sights one often encountered in France, such as drunks and *pissoirs*. I remember laughing uproariously at a drunk on a bicycle attempting to find his way home, but merely succeeding in falling off every few yards. The sight of the local bus losing its front wheel going round the *Place* left me in fits. Things like that simply did not happen in England.

My mother and John returned to France the following year, leaving me confined to bed with measles. My father, wanting to cheer me up, asked if there was a book I would like to read. I replied immediately,

Jocelyn Galsworthy

Peter May's Book of Cricket. Somewhat surprised, he went off to buy it, and I devoured it from cover to cover. When I had recovered, I joined John and my mother in France for another painting holiday.

In 1960, after a brief stay in Paris, my mother decided to take me to Germany in order to further my drawing. We stayed in a little village south of Munich called Schliersee, with a *Frau* von Hünnius, who

The Teutonic tutor, Peter Loew   pastel

centre of Munich. He did not speak any English and I no German, so I had to do a crash course in the language in order to communicate with him. I learnt German, but he refused to learn English. Peter Loew was talented and good-looking in a Teutonic kind of way, but I found him exasperating at times. It was 1960, and I was traditional and old-fashioned in outlook. Peter was rather too modern for my taste and he found me uninteresting. He

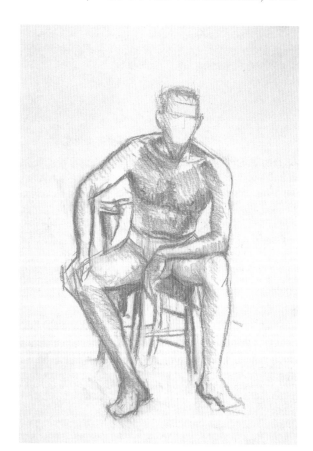

Life drawing of male nude

had been a great friend of my mother before the war in Riga. My mother had been teaching her daughter Cécile (now Baroness von Oelsen) English, but at the outbreak of the war in 1939 was urged to return to England at once. This she did, only resuming contact with the family again when the Red Cross managed to trace them. When my aunt and a friend arrived to stay with us, the Baroness offered her services as chauffeur, and drove us in her Volkswagen round the Munich countryside. Her driving was truly frightful and we all sat rigid with fear; even Tita the great talker, knowing no German, was silent for once.

A young tutor by the name of Peter Loew was found for me and I began life drawing with him at his studio in the

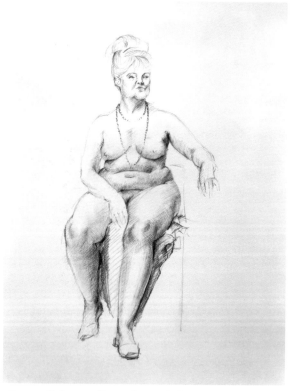

One of the well-endowed female nudes which caused embarrassment to German Customs

focused his attention instead on my glamorous mother, who rather reciprocated. Fortunately for everyone, she returned to England, but continued to write to him for some time after. He later became very well-known in his own country.

He taught me a great deal in spite of everything else going on around me, and I returned to England with acres of drawings rolled up in cardboard tubes. At Customs leaving Germany, an extremely officious woman officer with cropped hair and steely eyes, whom I disliked instantly, demanded to know what was in the cardboard tubes. I told her I was an art student and they were my drawings. She made me get them out and show her. Out came nudes of every shape and size drawn from life. Her face was a picture of embarrassment and her male counterparts, as well as passengers near by, all had a good look, barely suppressing their sniggers. It served her right.

On returning to England I went to the City and Guilds School of Art in Kennington which, in those days, was a

Rudo Sauter *pastel 1976*

very serious, hard-working establishment. I am afraid I simply did not get on with my fellow art students, who seemed to me to be lazy and dirty, with strange left-wing ideas which invariably conflicted with mine. I could not wait to be free of them. Rudo Sauter was asked by my father if he could recommend a portrait studio to which I could go for tuition. He put me in touch with Edward Halliday, the foremost portrait painter of his day (he painted Churchill, Nehru and most of the Royal Family several times over), who agreed to sit for me for a drawing. He recommended Kenneth Green RP who took a few students in his studio in St John's Wood. His working studio embraced all ages of student, but as I recollect, I was practically the only one striving to be a professional portrait painter. I was there for three months and enjoyed it greatly.

It was in 1961 that I first met Brian Johnston and his family. I was eighteen and John sixteen and that summer, my father's stockbroker came to stay at our cottage at Worth Matravers in Dorset. His sister, married to the MP for Poole, Sir Richard Pilkington, also had a house in Hamilton Terrace, St John's Wood, near the Johnstons. When they had a drinks party my parents were invited and Brian and Pauline were there too. John and I

A young Brian Johnston   *charcoal drawing 1961*

had been left in the car outside as the invitation had not been extended to us. My father brought Brian out to speak to us, knowing how thrilled we would be to meet him. Brian and Pauline asked us all to their cottage when we were next down in Dorset, and I received a commission for a painting of their cottage at Acton, the village next to Worth Matravers on the Isle of Purbeck. I was also fortunate enough to be able to do a drawing of Brian as, being the kind man he was, he agreed to sit for me. That was a great excitement in those days. My brother and I were so keen on cricket, that to meet and get to know the great man was something very special for us.

I spent a great deal of time painting and drawing the locals at Worth Matravers mostly using charcoal. They were great characters and were willing to sit for hours (if the truth be known that is what they did most days for most of the time).

In 1962 I returned to Spain by boat from Tilbury. I stayed in my cabin for the entire trip and never knew of the raging storm in the Bay of Biscay. I was met at Gibraltar by my cousins and taken to the

Bristol Hotel, where I was joined a few days later by Tessa Hankey, the daughter of my father's greatest friend. Luckily Tessa could drive, so we hired a car and drove all over the south of Spain. I painted whenever the mood took me, or something caught my eye, which was almost all the time, and it was here that my painting really began to flourish.

On our way to Granada, we stopped at Ronda. Our little hotel overlooked the mountains, and we used to sit on our balcony admiring the view. Tessa was forever being leered at or worse, which, not unnaturally, she heartily disliked. One morning, I left to go to mass very early while Tessa stayed in bed enjoying a lie-in. When I returned, I found the window tight shut, the curtains drawn and Tessa in a panic. Workmen were marching backwards and forwards from one balcony to another, in an attempt to catch a glimpse of the good-looking English girl. Unlike Tessa, I always shrugged off such attention, or responded with a few well-chosen words which always seemed to work.

I had lessons with the Head of the Granada Art School, *Señor* Revelles Lopez. He asked Tessa who was a very striking girl, to sit as a model so that he could do a demonstration portrait of her for my edification. He then made me paint her, and it turned out to be an excellent likeness which pleased *Señor* Lopez. Poor Tessa was patience personified, but even she had had enough by then.

This became one of the most revealing

and enlightening times of my artistic life. I was very young and innocent for my age and every day seemed a new adventure. Tessa was yet again extremely patient while I painted the locals. I was always asking people to sit for me, and sometimes, I would be surrounded by what seemed like the whole village until they were tired of watching me.

Tessa's brother was in the SCLI (Somerset and Cornwall Light Infantry) and introduced us to his brother officers. It is not hard to imagine the wonderful social life we had after that, much to the disapproval of my grandmother's aristocratic cousin Laurie, whose brother owned the hotel in which we were staying. We were of course nothing like as free as girls today, and behaved more like characters from a Jane Austen novel than liberated young women.

The Commanding Officer of the SCLI, Colonel Hine-Haycock, commissioned me to paint his daughter Daphne, aged eight. He and his wife, Felicity, had seen my work at a showing I had held in the only art shop in Gibraltar, and had liked what they had seen. I painted Daphne in the

Miguel   *oil on canvas*

Bristol Hotel where I was staying, and on the second day her mother came to see how things were progressing. She reported to her husband that evening that she thought they had made a terrible mistake. This is because pastel portraits in the initial stages do not resemble the finished work in any way. The underpainted face

appears as a vivid mixture of mauve, yellow and green, before the top coat, so to speak, is applied in normal skin tones. A pastel portrait is built up in layers and takes quite a time to look recognisable. In the event, however, they were thrilled with the portrait when it was finally finished.

The Hine-Haycocks became firm friends and after Gibraltar, when Colonel Hine-Haycock became CO at Shrewsbury, they invited me to stay and to paint him in his ceremonial uniform as well as their two eldest children, Rozanthe and Gerald. Gerald was about fifteen and had a passion for cycling. He dragged me all over Shrewsbury and the surrounding countryside, but I did not mind. Later I stayed with them in Kingswear, Devon, where they had a magnificent house, and I completed the family by painting Felicity.

While I was in Gibraltar David Shepherd, the celebrated artist, came out to paint the Colours Parade of the SCLI, to which Tessa and I were invited. I found myself sitting next to him at a dinner party that evening, which was very lucky for me, as he encouraged me to join the Chelsea Arts Society to which he belonged. I submitted work to their exhibitions for years afterwards. He impressed on me the fact that painting was very hard work – so many students regard it as a soft option. I remember him saying that in those days the first picture was for the gas bill, the second for the electricity and so on. He was very intolerant of artists who only painted when they felt like it. I found him to be a very modest man, and at that stage in my budding career I was very flattered that he had taken the time to discuss art with me.

In 1963 I returned to Spain, again with Tessa, taking the train through France, and staying with my cousins in Paris. Thence to Madrid, where I spent my twenty-first birthday, staying in a typically Spanish hotel, where the food was excellent and the service kindly and helpful. Four days in Madrid were not enough. It took me all that time to see the Prado, let alone anything else. I had always loved the Spanish masters, particularly Murillo and Velázquez, and would try to emulate them.

The Dowager Countess of Malmesbury   *oil on canvas*

The journey to Algeciras was like crossing the wild west, with spectacular, hot, barren countryside. We were glad we were not on foot but in our train which was clean and comfortable and had an excellent restaurant car, where we spent a considerable part of the journey.

On arrival in Gibraltar, we hired a car (I could drive by then), and I started taking commissions. I paid my way by painting, and even won a prize in Gibraltar when I entered a competition with a portrait of 'El Guardacoche'. I received a book from the Governor and also sold the portrait. I was elated at this humble success and it never occurred to me that I was perhaps taking commissions before I was ready. If people were willing to pay, I thought, I must be good enough. Looking back, although there were some good portraits, far too many were mediocre by my standards today. My very first portrait commission had come in 1960, when I painted a Mrs Ian Fraser, which I think was rather better than the portraits I did in Gibraltar at that time. My father was delighted that I had financially supported myself and for my twenty-first birthday gave me our house at Winchester. Unfortunately, my parents decided to stay put, so the gift was of no immediate advantage, but I was gratified by his confidence in me.

It was at this time that I made the

decision to concentrate on pastels. I had my heart set on being a portrait painter, specialising in children. Pastels were particularly suited to portraits of children I thought, because as everyone knows, they never sit still and with pastels it is possible to pick up after a gap without any detriment to the painting. I also found that pastels portrayed the texture of children's skin more realistically. In any case, I had always loved children and had even wanted to look after them at one time. I taught myself to use pastels by trial and error. I read all the books I could find on technique and simply got on with painting.

I decided to hold my first major exhibition in the Guildhall in Winchester in 1964, and my parents worked frantically to try and make it a success. They roped in everyone they knew to come and support me, which they did. My father, having lived in the area since 1924, knew everybody, including the Earl of Malmesbury, who became one of my very first patrons. My mother who got on very well with Lady Malmesbury, wrote to her asking her to help in any way she could to promote my work, whereupon I was immediately commissioned to paint the Dowager Countess of Malmesbury. She came to my studio at home and was the easiest of sitters. A great gardener, she was at once enthralled by my mother's roses, and thoroughly enjoyed the company of my father, who came to entertain her. Afterwards, she became a constant guest at dinner. Although in her eighties, she was so young at heart that all my contemporaries loved her. The portrait was a great success, and to this day hangs in Lord Malmesbury's house. I was then twenty-two and it was a very important commission.

The same year I travelled to Paris to stay with my French cousins and did many drawings all over the city, setting myself up in the street. The French, who know they are a very artistic nation, are full of opinions, and like to give one advice. I was painting the Pont Neuf, when a Frenchman came up to me, praised the bridge and offered to show me how to paint the sky, which he told me was lousy! Within five minutes, a complete stranger had told me how to get the clouds right. Something similar happened on another visit to Paris, when an elderly man offered to help me with my oil painting. He told me that he had a studio not far away. Innocent that I was, I never suspected an ulterior motive and, fortunately, on that occasion, all was above board, but it could have turned out very differently. I attended classes in his attic studio with six other would-be artists and, as luck would have it, they were all highly respectable.

Chapter 3   London Beckons

*I*t was in 1964, due to one of those quirks of fate which become a turning point in one's life, that I settled in London. The couple who had rented the house at the bottom of our drive at Winchester asked me to paint a portrait of their niece, whose parents, Dorrien and Mary Belson, lived at Kensington Gate. I was happy to oblige, and struck up a friendship with the child's parents. By a stroke of good fortune, Mary's sister, Anne Biddle, and her husband Donald, had just bought a house with a basement flat in

First Street, Chelsea. 'How would you like an artist for your basement?' Mary asked, as though you were nobody unless you had one. The suggestion seemed to go down well with the Biddles and I became their tenant, relishing the thought of independence at last. This idea did not sit very well with my father, who did not want me to leave home even though I was in my twenties. If I ever stayed with anyone and did not return on the day I had said I would, I was sure to be in trouble. I was never free, and felt as if I was ruled with

a rod of iron, but a sense of duty compelled me to put up with it.

My mother had started having bouts of depression and I was needed at home more than ever. However, I had my own life and career to consider, but this did not stop me feeling guilty at putting my own interests ahead of those of my parents. The family friction caused by my decision to live in London, at least during the week, did nothing for my development as an artist. Perhaps as an antidote to her depressive moods, my mother started to take her own painting seriously and this helped her enormously during the awful years when she went undiagnosed as a manic-depressive.

Her own painting career subsequently flourished. She held many highly acclaimed exhibitions, some jointly with me, and by the end of her life (she died in August 1998), her vibrant flower paintings were selling widely and commanding ever-increasing prices. She was a remarkable woman with whom I had a very special bond, and whose influence will always be with me. However, at this stage, in the grip of an illness which is more often than not misunderstood, she was powerless to placate my father, and to smooth my transition from dutiful daughter to independent woman. Thank goodness for London, where I had a great deal of fun with my new-found friends. I played bridge as often as I could, and became an energetic Scottish dancer. One

JG painting in the street in London

of my friends, who had been at Twyford Prep School with my brother, shared a flat with four others in Redcliffe Square. They, and others, were always on hand to escort me to dances. I never found myself without male company, but it was far too early for me to think of settling down with one person. In any case, my mother always likened marriage to glorified housekeeping, and I felt I had had quite enough of that. I would rather wait and see what turned up, while concentrating on my painting which I found all-absorbing. If the truth be known, I was looking for someone very special. He had to be rich (and preferably titled), understanding, gallant, old-fashioned and fun. Does such a man exist? If he does, I have not yet found him and if I did find him, he would probably not want me!

At weekends I went home where my parents entertained royally. In the summer there were tennis parties on our beautifully-kept grass court, my father's pride and joy, and these tennis gatherings were usually followed by a dinner party. My mother was a consummate hostess and cooked wonderfully well, in a

'A Floral Symphony'   *oil on canvas*
Yvette Galsworthy

completely untaught way. My parents were very generous with their hospitality, and wine flowed, inducing lively conversation. We had no taboos about religion or politics and these subjects were freely and hotly debated at the dinner table. I think my love of controversy stems from that time, but nowadays people feel insulted when one expresses the opposite view,

and debate is very often stifled. I like to argue forcefully with my friends, but this does not imply any hostility. Sex was rarely, if ever, mentioned and to this day I feel quite uncomfortable with uninhibited talk of an explicit nature, which strangely enough does not put people off in anything like the same way as politics or religion.

In a minor way I also became very involved in politics. Whenever elections, whether local or general, came up, I was to be seen canvassing for the Conservatives in the more run-down areas of London such as North Kensington or Shepherd's Bush. These areas are probably fashionable today, but in the sixties the reverse was true. I cannot recall how many doors were slammed in my face or how many scathing remarks I endured, but I must have developed a tough outer hide which has stood me in good stead, as I am not easily put off by failure. There was a lighter side – I was roped in to paint the decor for a Conservative fund-raiser, The Top Gear Ball, held at a London hotel. It was tremendous fun. I painted sheets and sheets of Paris street scene with poster paints on a dark blue background with which we covered the walls. It worked well and looked very romantic.

About this time a friend and I did a meals-on-wheels round, taking food to those who could not look after themselves. My friend, great fun but rather scatty, drove the van and we raced round London (continually making up for lost time) with trays of meat and two veg for the unfortunate elderly and infirm. On one occasion we skidded to a halt and one of the trays shot out of the back door of the van, the contents ending up on the road. 'Never mind,' said my friend, 'We'll scoop it up and put it back and give it to old Mrs X [who was blind]. She'll never know!' It horrifies me now to think how politically incorrect we were. We felt we had to do our bit for society, but not too seriously.

Maurice Green, then editor of *The Daily Telegraph*, and his wife had bought a cottage very near our house at Winchester. They became great friends of my parents, and once again my mother found another man irresistible. She was seduced by his intellect and love of music, and lit up whenever he was around. History does not relate how far this

Maurice Green   *charcoal drawing*

passion went. I asked him if I could do a charcoal drawing of him and he accepted. I submitted it to The Royal Society of Portrait Painters in 1967 when they were still at the RBA Galleries behind the Haymarket, where, in those days pastels and drawings were given much more prominence. The drawing received complimentary reviews which was very flattering. The Royal Society of Portrait Painters moved to The Mall Galleries and

unfortunately, the ratio of pastels and drawings to oils decreased substantially. There is an obvious prejudice against pastels by the Selection Committee and large, fully painted work is seldom accepted. I sometimes think they forget that it is The Royal Society of Portrait Painters, not the Royal Society of Portrait Painters in Oils.

One of a portrait painter's greatest assets, I feel, is the ability to get on with all sorts of people, even under difficult circumstances. The artist must always be in control, combining tact with firmness, otherwise the painting can end up pleasing neither the sitter nor the artist. I never alter my portraits unless I agree that there is a glaring fault. I strive for a good likeness, plenty of character and an accomplished painting. The character and likeness must be truly representative, but not necessarily to the sitter. I have been blessed with the ability to get a good likeness, far more difficult than painting landscapes, but I do not mind constructive criticism. All too often, however, I receive uninformed comments which are not helpful. My father, mother, aunt and, latterly, my brother were my most severe critics, but always in a

My brother John   *oil on canvas 1967*

Tom Duke   *oil on canvas*

Siegfried Sassoon charcoal drawing
Tita kept him entertained while I drew.

Lieutenant Roberts VC charcoal drawing

Rear-Admiral Sir Anthony Miers VC, KBE, CB, DSO and Bar   *pastel*

constructive way. This gave me the confidence I needed to deal with clients. I am also very gregarious and love being with people, which I have found a great asset in my painting life.

In the fullness of time, Anne and Donald Biddle decided to move to the country, to Sussex not far from East Grinstead. How I wished I could have bought their First Street house as a studio, but my father would not hear of it. In the end it went for the now ridiculous sum of £27,000, but it might as well have been £27,000,000 since there was no way I could afford that or anything else. I felt that my painting life was set back a good few years because, instead of being able to concentrate on my work, I became involved with the lives of the families I lived with, rewarding though that was. Luckily, I was asked to go with my friends to Sussex and have the cottage in the garden. It was a consolation to be with such good people, as my home life was not happy. My parents were in difficulties and drifting apart, and there seemed to be no end to my mother's depression.

My first major commission now came my way through the good offices of the headmaster of my brother's old prep school, Twyford. He knew the Curator of HMS *Dolphin,* the submariner museum at Gosport, and recommended me when they wanted to commission drawings of fifteen submariners who had received Victoria Crosses during both world wars. These drawings attracted a great deal of publicity and I was very proud to have been chosen for this task. Admiral Sir Anthony Miers, who was one of the VCs, subsequently became a friend and I was asked to do a portrait of Lady Miers. When he died, she asked me to paint a full length posthumous portrait of him in his full dress naval uniform. I remember that the detail on his innumerable medals gave me immense trouble. If I had been painting in oils, and using a brush, I could have achieved greater definition in a shorter time.

Eventually, I moved out of the cottage and into the big house with Anne and Donald, where I was given a studio. By this time there were two boys, Justin and Mark, whom I helped to care for. I was now able to combine my two loves, painting and children, and this was a very happy time for me.

I would go to Warminster regularly to stay with my aunt, and I produced many paintings using her house as a base. Siegfried Sassoon was a great friend of Tita, and I visited him at Heytesbury House, where my aunt kept him

Jocelyn Galsworthy

entertained while I did a drawing of him. I later sold it to the Head of Manuscripts at Sotheby's, who was a collector of literary portraits, but not before I had made a copy for Sassoon himself who liked my drawing and presented it to his parish priest.

My mother, who had decided to become a 'proper artist', had taken herself off to the South of France, and when she had amassed enough canvasses for an exhibition, held her first *vernissage* at the casino in Monte Carlo. The family went to support her, including myself, and I stayed on with her. My father had been on his boat on the River Dart while my mother went on her painting trips and it had worked out quite well.

I continued to live happily in Sussex, as part of an enlarging family, but I really ought to have been painting more. Twin girls, Georgina and Anne-Marie, arrived in 1972 so there were now four children under five years old and I was virtually indispensable. My father was not amused as my painting took more and more of a back seat. I already had a number of exhibitions to my credit, starting with the Guildhall in Winchester in 1964, and for the next four years I showed at various London galleries. These years were very productive from the point of view of commissions.

One of my earliest portraits (done in oils) was of Anne Biddle. The way it came about was rather amusing. Anne and Donald had gone away to the Mexico Olympics, and very foolishly allowed me to use their brand-new Rover. Owing to a lack of judgement on my part, I scraped the length of the car whilst squeezing through a non-existent gap. Knowing that I would never be able to pay for the repairs, they asked me for a full length portrait in oils by way of compensation. I was relieved to be able to oblige, and happily they were thrilled with the painting and still have it hanging in their house.

When I passed my driving test in 1962 (waiting for John to be able to take his) my father lent us his old 1948 Land Rover which I drove all over the place. John by this time had gone to America. When I moved to Sussex the Land Rover came with me and I drove to London with Anne. Halfway there, the front wheel suddenly detached itself and rolled away, leaving us stranded. A catalogue of disasters with the Land Rover followed, costing me a great deal of money, but Tita took pity on me and bought me a new Morris Marina. I sold the Land Rover to the Biddles to use on the estate. My father was furious with me and never let up until the end of his life. The

Anne Biddle   oil on canvas 1968
This portrait was swapped for car repairs.

Marina turned out to be unsuitable for my purposes, so I exchanged it for a later model of Land Rover, which gave me many years of reliable service and became my outdoor studio and trademark. All my charges loved to be collected in the Land Rover as it was considered 'cool'. When I left Sussex I bought the old Land Rover back, had it restored and returned it to my father, thinking to please him. He immediately sold it.

In 1970 I held a joint exhibition with my mother and father in Birmingham. My father exhibited some of his pen and ink drawings, done while accompanying my mother abroad. These little sketches were accomplished, well-composed and executed, and a number of them sold.

My mother (ever on the look out for a more exciting life) started cooking directors' lunches in 1974 for a PR firm in Covent Garden. She stayed in a flat above the offices, and being right opposite the Opera House, would queue for the gods whenever the mood took her. The PR firm somehow became involved in a London showing for my mother and myself which we had decided to hold in

Judy and Charlie   *pastel 1978*

aid of the Spastics' Society of which Dorrien Belson was Chairman. It was to be held at the Chenil Galleries in King's Road, where Augustus John used to exhibit in his heyday. The French Resistance heroine, Odette Hallowes GC, was asked to open it which attracted a

great deal of publicity, and resulted in many portrait commissions. I was by now becoming much more confident about my ability as a portrait painter, and tackled these new commissions with enthusiasm.

After two further exhibitions, in Winchester and East Grinstead, I again teamed up with my mother in 1977 when she exhibited the first of the flower paintings which were to become her hallmark for the next twenty-six years. On this occasion I concentrated on landscapes and portraits.

When I moved to Sussex with Anne and Donald, I was kept extremely busy for the first few years, but by the time the boys had gone to school, Tita began to feel that I should live in London during the week at least, in order to further my portrait painting career. A friend of Anne and Donald offered to let me stay in her house in Old Church Street, Chelsea, from which I could undertake London commissions and in 1978 I held an exhibition there. My aunt was of the opinion that paintings look better in private houses and she may have had a point. My friends had erected a marquee

The Hurst family   *pastel*

Sir Geraint Evans   *sepia drawing 1980*

for me in the garden and had created such a glamorous atmosphere that I felt sure it would be a success. It was, and I acquired several valuable portrait commissions on the strength of it. I can honestly say that from that moment my career began to expand. I also matured as a person and gradually began to stand on my own two feet.

At about this time I decided that I must have a collection of portraits of distinguished people to exhibit. I wrote to many musicians, singers and actors, among them Vladimir Ashkenazy, Lennox Berkeley, Geraint Evans, Janet Baker, Esmond Knight and Nyree Dawn Porter. Nyree Dawn Porter, of course, had portrayed Irene in The Forsyte Saga on television. Louis Kentner, who was married to Yehudi Menuhin's wife's sister, agreed instantly when I asked him to sit for me, but sadly, Yehudi Menuhin did not. Dame Janet was so pleased with her portrait that she bought it, but in the main they were for my own collection. Of course, any artist, especially an impecunious one, is always glad to sell.

My father became very ill with cancer of the spine which was only diagnosed in January 1978 and kept from all of us except his sister Tita. It progressed very rapidly and he died in July of that year. The flood of letters we received testified to the warmth of feeling of his friends. He had been part of Winchester life for fifty years: a great ladies' man before the war, an accomplished sportsman, a brilliant dancer and lively conversationalist. I shared his love of the sea, tennis and cricket and found him great company when we were on our own. He was, however, a very difficult father; intolerant to a degree, always demanding the highest standards of his children and over-reacting when he was thwarted. My father's death was a worrying time for my mother, who did not like being on her own, so after a while she decided to live with Tita in Warminster. Tita converted the attic for her, which my mother loved, as she adored the Bohemian life and could imagine herself in Paris while she painted. Meanwhile, I rented a flat in Knightsbridge and took small classes of children for drawing lessons. It proved to be a big mistake, as I discovered I hated teaching, and the parents were too demanding. I also resented not being able to paint while I was teaching.

As my mother had decided to move, our family house at Winchester was sold in 1980. With the proceeds I bought my very own flat off Tedworth Square, which

My father   *sepia drawing 1975*

I sold in 1983 when a good offer came along. It was only in 1988 that I again ventured into the property market. I bought a house on the Isle of Wight where I now have a studio, and I have also acquired the house next door to give me more room for painting. In the first years of having my little house, my godchildren

used to come and stay. (They always called me 'Dozey' because when I was nowhere to be found I was invariably asleep, sunning myself, in the rose garden). I once had twenty-two young people for the Bembridge Ball sleeping everywhere. I used to do Cadet Week with my young charges in years gone by at the Bembridge Sailing Club, and taking the opportunity to paint the wonderful seascapes on the Isle of Wight, I used to exhibit at the Club along with Cavendish Morton, the distinguished marine artist. Unfortunately, I did not find it an ideal venue as we were unable to attract enough new blood to the exhibition. However, I still get all my framing done by the gallery in Bembridge.

Another exhibition was held in 1979, again at Old Church Street, and in 1980 at the Fortescue Swann Gallery in Old Brompton Road. In 1982 I joined up with my mother again for a showing at the Chelsea Town Hall and this time it was she who had tremendous sales. It has been said, perhaps as a criticism, that as our two styles were so very different, it was not a good idea to hang our pictures

Jocelyn Galsworthy

Bembridge-View of St.Helen's Fort and the lifeboat station from the Duver

pastel

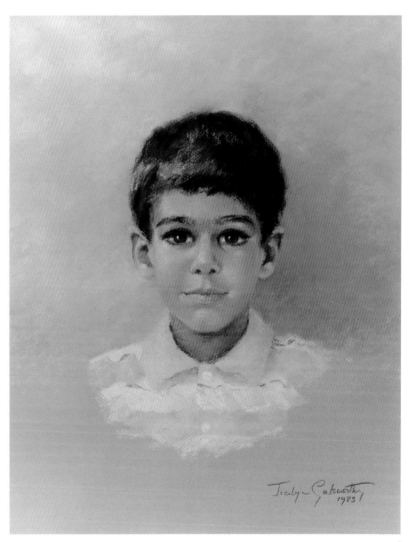

pastel

pastel

Two portraits in pastel of the children I so love to paint

together. My mother's paintings are dramatic and flamboyant, vibrant with colour, whereas mine are delicate as befits pastel, although always fully painted with more depth of colour than is usual with that medium. The critics may have been right, but I always enjoyed our joint efforts and it gave my mother so much pleasure.

At the time of the Gulf War, I again joined my mother in France for a painting holiday, the results of which we exhibited in the autumn of 1982 at Chelsea Town Hall. Shortly afterwards my mother became seriously ill and went into a nursing home in London and my grandmother, who could no longer live on her own, decided to move in with

'Tulips' *oil on canvas*
Yvette Galsworthy

me. We got on very well, but following a fall which broke her arm she needed full-time nursing. She returned to Hove and moved into a residential club with nursing. She talked her way in, insisting that she was only temporarily laid up and that once her arm had healed she would be as active as all the other residents. She looked seventy and was accepted, although in reality she was ninety. She lived to be one hundred and two, and my poor mother, who visited her often, was exhausted by her. It always amused me to hear my mother tell people that she was going to Hove to visit her mother. They thought she must have lost her marbles, as most eighty-year-olds do not have a parent still living.

Chapter 4   A Proper Artist

The Guards' Cricket Club, Burton Court

pastel

When I started painting portraits, it was often easier to stay with people than ask them to visit me, since I did not have a permanent studio. My father had said that portrait painting could be a marvellous life, staying in grand houses and being well looked after, while earning a living doing what one loved. It may well have been so before the war, but today I find Noel Coward's witty 'Stately Homes of England' much nearer the mark -'The lavatory used by Charles the First (quite informally) and later George the Fourth on the journey north . . .' The houses are mostly freezing because they never have the central heating on. The food is barely passable and there is never enough of it. I had a very healthy appetite then, as now, and usually went to bed hungry. After a day's painting I was often completely exhausted, and the last thing I wanted to do was to be on my best behaviour, make stilted conversation and help with the drying up. Beds were often damp and I did not sleep very well.

One of my happy memories, by contrast, is of my stay at Kedleston, that perfect example of an Adam house, to paint the Scarsdale family. Here, tradition and old-fashioned standards prevailed, much to my delight.

In general I made up my mind that after my prices reached a significant level, I would stay in a decent hotel nearby instead. I did meet some wonderful people, of course, who have remained long-standing friends.

I well remember going to one family in February. The child was extremely badly behaved, the parents never got out of bed, and the turkey I was given to eat must have been in the 'fridge, since Christmas. However, they were quite pleased with the portrait. After about ten years of that sort of treatment, I had had enough. Stories of some of the families I have stayed with would make a fascinating book, but I fear I would not be very popular.

I do not know why it took me so long to get around to painting cricket. As early as 1965 I had painted a cricket match in oils at St Cross, the Free Foresters v I Zingari.[3] But, it was not until 1983 that I attempted my next effort. I painted a prep school match between

Sir William Becher Bt. MC   *pastel 1985*

Summerfields and Cheam as part of my collection for my next exhibition which would be called 'Public Schools and Present Headmasters'. Next I painted at

St. Malo, Brittany   *pastel*

Yvette, my mother   *conté drawing*

Burton Court, the Guards' Cricket Club in Chelsea, where I saw Lady Becher who asked me to do a portrait of her husband, Sir William, for his seventieth birthday. I duly appeared at their house with my albums to show them my work and they were amused to see the pictures of Lord Malmesbury and his mother. It turned out that they were cousins. As Sir William was Secretary of I Zingari at the time, we talked cricket non-stop, and he suggested I paint the Centenary Match between IZ and the Royal Green Jackets' Cricket Club (RGJCC) at St Cross, Winchester, in 1985. This I did, and from that time on I never looked back. The Green Jackets bought the original which hangs in their Mess and Colonel Elliott, Secretary of the RGJCC, bought all the limited edition prints I had made of the match. Cricket now reasserted itself as my great love and, being a portrait painter and keen on figure drawing, the two fitted together perfectly. I had found my niche.

However, I continued and still continue, to do seascapes and landscapes as well as portraits as I consider it important to be as varied as possible. I paint on the Isle of Wight where I now have my permanent home, and enjoy the ever-changing moods of the sea. The harbour near my house and the yachts of all sizes provide an endless source of material. The light is dramatic and always changing so that the same scene can appear completely different depending on the time of day. This often happens on the coast, particularly when the sun is behind, intensifying the natural colours.

The contacts I made preparing for the 'Public Schools and Present Headmasters' exhibition have been very important to me even to this day. Dennis Silk, Warden of Radley at the time and a great cricketer,

Yvonne, my mother's sister   *pastel*
(always called 'Baba')

became President of the MCC. He has always been extremely friendly and helpful and has watched my progress very closely. Similarly, Donald Fowler-Watt, then Headmaster of Brambletye Prep School, a more than enthusiastic, some would say fanatical, cricketer together with his wife has purchased and commissioned my work several times and has supported me in every way he could.

Shortly after this exhibition, I was commissioned to draw John Whittaker,

Headmaster of Sussex House Prep School, by the mother of a pupil there, on behalf of the parents. John Whittaker was a mad keen cricketer, had been in the Green Jackets and played for the Sussex Martlets.

In 1986 I held a major exhibition at the school through John's kindness, which was by far my most successful to date. It comprised almost all cricket paintings and portraits. Some time earlier I had drawn the writer and journalist Peregrine Worsthorne, who agreed to open this exhibition. He had a great following, which swelled the numbers enormously.

Dennis Silk CBE   *sepia drawing*

John had worked tirelessly to make it a success, and looking round the jam-packed room I felt truly gratified. It was a sell-out and set me on the right road to the world of cricket which is where I feel I belong. That evening, two cricket paintings were bought by Lord and Lady Annaly whom I had briefly met on another occasion. I was commissioned to paint a portrait of Lord Annaly at his country house in Hampshire and also Cadogan Square where they had their London flat. They also commissioned a painting of the Evie Hone window in Eton College Chapel for a Christmas card to be sold in aid of the Anastasia Trust for the Deaf, which Lady Annaly had founded. Sadly, Lord Annaly died soon after, but his widow, Beverley, has become a firm friend and supporter of my work and I am a great admirer of her ceaseless activity on

behalf of her charities. Her unfailing *joie de vivre* and optimism are both an encouragement and an example.

I did my first painting of Arundel in 1986. This fabulous ground in Sussex was created by the late Duke of Norfolk, a great cricketer and manager of the MCC on many overseas tours. It is in the shape of an amphitheatre, with the Catholic cathedral beyond the trees. It has a wonderful pavilion and, deservedly, a huge membership – The Friends of Arundel Castle Cricket Club. It has always been a tradition that the first match of any home Test series is staged here, the only exception being in 1994 when the South Africans returned to international cricket. On this occasion, Lord Carnarvon at Highclere pipped them to the post. People can drive their cars to the edge of

John Whittaker, Sir Peregrine Worsthorne and Jocelyn Galsworthy at the opening of my 1986 exhibition at Sussex House

Photo J. Cazals

Sir Peregrine Worsthorne   *sepia drawing*

Stowe School   *pastel*

Agar's, Eton College

pastel

Jocelyn Galsworthy

Harrow School   *pastel*

the boundary at Arundel which is a real boon to the elderly, who can spend the day there with their picnics and enjoy top class club and county cricket. There are very few rules, and no-one would dream of infringing them.

Hubert Doggart, a great cricketer in his time and a thoroughly accomplished after dinner speaker, has been the Chairman of the Friends of Arundel Castle Cricket Club for many years. His son was master of cricket at Eton and they were all very helpful to me when I began painting cricket seriously.

My other favourite ground is Burton Court in Chelsea, sandwiched between the Royal Hospital and St Leonard's Terrace. The bands of the various Guards regiments playing under the trees during tea give the ground a special atmosphere. I have always been royally treated there, and made to feel most welcome. When I first painted at Burton Court, Colonel Malcolm Havergal was Chairman of the Guards' Cricket Club and his wife Fiona, a great gardener, used to tend the Club's wonderful roses. They were welcoming, hospitable and supportive and have remained

The Lord Annaly   *pastel*

so. I have painted Burton Court six times from all angles and there always seems to be a demand for pictures of this beautiful London ground. On one occasion, when Tom King, the former Minister of Defence, was batting for the Lords and Commons, he hit a tremendous six which nearly landed on top of me. Gallantly, the

Guards' Club at once put a fielder on the boundary to protect me – it is definitely not safe to park your car near Burton Court on cricket days. The Club has a very full fixture list with public schools, regiments, politicians and charities, keeping the admirable Christian Muteau, their indefatigable scorer, busy all season.

My first painting of The Oval was of the Lords v the Commons, the first such match for many years. As they had shortened the boundary, I was allowed to take my easel on to the outfield. The Oval is one of the largest cricket grounds in the world and for private matches they bring the boundary right in, as otherwise it would be too remote. At that time, the pavilion had not been refurbished and was not a thing of beauty. I made prints of my finished painting which now is of some historic interest as the refurbishment completely changed the landscape.

In 1987, the great friends in whose house I had had a studio for the last few years in London, bought a large house outside Ascot and offered me the annexe. I once again had to decide whether to stay in London without a roof, or go back to

The Guards' Cricket Club, Burton Court with the roses in bloom

pastel

Cricket at Ludgrove School

pastel

Gemini v IZ (Australia) Sunningdale School

pastel

the country with people I knew. I chose the latter, but inevitably I was side-tracked, by horses this time, as my friend showed extensively, and painting took a bit of a back seat.

My 1988 exhibition was held at Sunningdale School run by the Dawson twins, which is one of the few family schools still in existence and where Brian Johnston sent his sons. The Dawson twins also run Gemini, the cricket club started by their father when they were born. The exhibition was opened by Lord MacLean whom I had met when I was painting Clarence House and St James's a few years earlier. I was very honoured when Lord MacLean, the Lord Chamberlain, bought my painting of Clarence House as a gift for Queen Elizabeth The Queen Mother for her birthday.

Two years later, my mother decided it was time to show her flower paintings again, having amassed quite a collection since her last exhibition. She asked me to join her, which as ever, I was delighted to do. We exhibited at the Ebury Court Hotel, which was a large undertaking as it was not a gallery or normal venue for showing works of art. This proved to be a costly mistake for although we sold well, the cost and aggravation outweighed any benefit to us.

When I eventually decided that painting cricket was going to be my destiny, I set myself a punishing schedule. Much to my friends' amazement, I stuck to it all summer. I would leave the house around 5.30 a.m., not reappearing until 11 p.m. in the evening. A quick supper, bed and off again. I was tired, but never let that stop me. I was determined to succeed, even if it did mean ungodly hours, and driving the length and breadth of the British Isles.

In September 1992 I held an exhibition on my own in Eton. I had booked a gallery and was let down at the last minute, but fortunately was able to reorganise it a few doors down. This had never happened to me before, and caused me untold inconvenience, since I did not know until the very last minute whether the exhibition could go ahead. Unbeknown to me the Mayor of the Royal Borough of Windsor and Maidenhead decided to pay a visit to the Private View. His limousine drew up outside the little shop in the high street, and with much ceremony, his Worship was announced. He entered, resplendent in his chain of office, and I am afraid I took not the slightest notice, my back being turned at the time as I was deep in conversation. He did a quick tour and left, the limousine gliding away into the night. History does not record what he thought of my pictures.

The following year I asked permission to do a painting of the cricket ground at Highclere, which, luckily for me, Lord Carnarvon liked so much that his Estate Manager, Tim Howland, then commissioned me to paint the opening match between The Earl of Carnarvon's XI and South Africa at Highclere in June 1994. It was remarkable how they transformed the ground without compromising the rural feel and were able to accommodate the thousands who had bought tickets. David Gower captained Lord Carnarvon's side, but they were soundly beaten which showed that the South Africans, for all their years in exile, had not lost their touch. It was a very memorable day, made more so by the incomparable setting and the presence of the Queen.

The Cricketer International reported the match and gave me excellent pictorial coverage. In fact, I would say that my debut into international cricket dated from this occasion. The organisers took all the prints I had made of the match and had them signed by Lord Carnarvon, David Gower and Kepler Wessels. I was then commissioned by Colonel John Stephenson (just retired as Secretary of the MCC) to paint the Test Match England v South Africa at Lord's.

In the autumn of that year, John Whittaker's last as Headmaster of Sussex House, I held another exhibition there devoted mostly to cricket. It was opened by Lord Deedes and Ted Dexter spoke on behalf of the Lord's Taverners. I had asked Brian Johnston to sit for a portrait, but, sadly, he died before he could do so. However, with Pauline Johnston's permission I painted a posthumous portrait of him to hang in the exhibition. This portrait

The Earl of Carnavon's XI v South Africa at Highclere, 1994   *pastel*

Charterhouse School

pastel

Jocelyn Galsworthy

Lord Deedes   _(Photo Sound Stills)_
Opening my 1994
Exhibition.

Ted Dexter speaking on   _(Photo Sound_
behalf of the Lord's Taverners   _Stills)_

The Rt. Hon. The Lord   _sepia drawing_
Deedes MC, PC, DL

Brian Johnston, MC   _pastel_
Now hanging in the Museum at Lord's.

was bought by the MCC and now resides in the refurbished museum at Lord's. Happily, the exhibition was a huge success, packed out and rewarding in terms of commissions and sales. Apart from cricket, my other love is golf and I exhibited several paintings of golf courses at Sussex House and received commissions to paint more.

I first met Lord Deedes at dinner with Gerald and Sue Bristowe, who had earlier bought and commissioned cricket paintings of Charterhouse. At Gerald's

suggestion, I was painting the links course at Littlestone in Kent. It was mid-December, a howling wind came straight off the sea and, for much of the time, I was huddled over my painting underneath my golf umbrella. Lord Deedes and Gerald found me in this state when they were playing the course. I do not know how I completed that painting, but it was an inspiring and rugged scene and was eventually bought by the Club. I later asked Lord Deedes whether he would sit for a portrait. He willingly agreed and I stayed

with Lord and Lady Deedes at their house at Ashford. He is the most amazing, knowledgeable man, with stamina second only to the Queen Mother, and a delight to talk to.

My first golf painting was of Ham, Richmond, followed by a painting from the second tee at Swinley Forest looking back towards the clubhouse. Swinley Forest is the most select golf club in the country, founded in the reign of Queen Victoria by Lord Derby. Women are still not allowed to play at weekends, which is probably why when a golf ball suddenly landed at my feet (I was painting amid the pine trees, well away from the fairway), its owner collected it without a look or a word in my direction.

I painted Royal Blackheath, which is over two hundred years old, and also Rochester and Cobham as well as twice depicting Stoke Poges with its beautiful clubhouse and the surrounding gardens laid out by Capability Brown. It was very pleasing to see that these were being restored to their former glory. I thought that Stoke Poges, in particular, would make an ideal limited edition print. This commission came after the 1994 exhibition in London, but it is very difficult for me to find the time to fit in painting golf. It is much more difficult to choose the best vantage point from which to paint on a golf course than on a cricket ground. Access is never easy and you need to know the course well. I also produced a painting of the golf course at Sunningdale and had introductions to courses in Scotland.

One day Nick Dawson, Joint Headmaster of Sunningdale School, came over to where I was painting the St Cross ground and a match between Gemini and the Royal Green Jackets, and informed me he had a project for me. 'I want you to paint the fives courts,' he said. I had never seen a game of Eton fives let alone understood the rules. I was quite dismayed at what I would have to paint – three concrete walls. Sunningdale has been fives prep school champions for many years and Nick said he would set up a match. It was a chilly October day and I felt I had my work cut out trying to make something attractive out of three concrete walls. The boys were most interested and one little chap came up to me and said, 'I've seen you at Mr Getty's ground and I've

Fives at Sunningdale School   *pastel*

seen you at St Cross and I've seen you at Highclere'. He was called Nicholas Oldridge and turned out to be Brian Johnston's grandson. Nicholas was very forthcoming and said he would like to see photos of the grounds I'd painted. The next day I brought my album. Nicholas and his little friends clustered round and Nicholas explained to them in the innocent, over-enthusiastic way that children have, 'This is a brilliant artist, she paints cricket all over the place. She's absolutely brilliant!' I will never forget it. I grew several inches that day. On telling his mother what a charming son she had, she said that he was very shy and never speaks to anyone. He was in the First XI at Stowe at a young age and Brian would be thrilled to think he was doing so well at the sport he loved. I finished the fives match and Nick Dawson was delighted with it, as he was with the prints I had made, which we sold to the parents.

I was asked to do two paintings of the shooting ground at Bisley. This was a most unusual commission for me, but John de Havilland, Chairman of the NRA, wanted me to paint a special match with himself in the foreground. This time I had to take photographs from which to work

Littlestone Golf Course

pastel

Swinley Forest Golf Club

pastel

The Royal Mid-Surrey Golf Course

pastel

Stoke Poges Golf Club

pastel

Shooting at Bisley   *pastel*

but that particular painting turned out, in my opinion, to be dramatic and beautiful. However, I found the constant noise disturbing and not conducive to painting, and for that reason could never really enthuse over painting anything connected with shooting.

Paul Sheldon, Director of the 150th Anniversary of The Oval (1995 was their anniversary year), commissioned me to do a Conversation Piece in oils on behalf of the Surrey County Cricket Club. The idea was that people paid to be in the painting, the funds going towards cricket coaching for young children in the deprived areas of London. This marvellous idea had been dreamed up by a Committee Member, Michael Soper.

I started the painting at the end of the cricket season that year, taking my easel to the outfield and endeavouring to pin down the vast six foot by ten foot canvas which the stiff breeze had made like a ship in full sail. I filled in the background, painted it all and kept it in one of the chalets at the Vauxhall end.

Surrey were in turmoil at that time and the 1995 anniversary year was soured by internal strife. Michael Soper, who had taken over the administration of the painting, was then made Chairman of the Club. He was too involved in other things to see to the painting and its administration so an aspiring committee member was appointed in his place. I found the publicity given to the painting inadequate and there were simply not enough people coming forward for me to put in which meant that it was very difficult for me to have any sort of structured composition. I was depressed and the whole project gave me little pleasure. However, I persevered (as I always do) and it has now suddenly come together. Having the administrative side of things now directly under my control has made an enormous difference. For once I broke my own golden rule about not painting from photographs, as it would have been impossible to get all those people to give me a sitting. I hope it will be considered a faithful representation of those in it, and of some historic interest in the years to come.

John Major (when he was Prime Minister) is in the foreground, as is E. W. Swanton, the oldest living member at The Oval. Peter May, who would have been President in 1995, sadly died in January that year and has been put in posthumously. Alec Stewart is there and all the Surrey/England greats, as well as many of the old players and the wonderful people who have paid to appear. When it is finally unveiled and hanging in the Long Room, I shall be immensely proud.

In that same year of 1994 I also painted the Cricketer Cup at Vincent Square. Belinda Brocklehurst and her husband Ben, owner of *The Cricketer International*, came to my exhibition at Sussex House and were very taken with the portraits. The Cricketer Cup is a competition for ex-public school boys, managed by their old schools, with matches held all over the country, culminating in

'Conversation Piece' (incomplete) 150th Anniversary Painting, Surrey County Cricket Club   *oil on canvas*

Cricketer Cup Final, Vincent Square, 1994   *pastel*

Belinda Brocklehurst   *pastel*

Ben Brocklehurst   *pastel*

Hampshire Hogs Cricket Club, Warnford   *pastel*

Upper Club, Eton College

pastel

Meads, Winchester College. A favourite ground

pastel

Sir Paul Getty's Ground at Wormsley   *pastel*

the final, now held at the Bank of England ground at Roehampton. It is a great occasion run entirely by *The Cricketer International*. The magazine also runs the schools Colts competition, with the final at Trent Bridge, and the Village Competition for the whole of the British Isles, culminating in a final at Lord's. It is extremely hard work to keep these competitions going and to find sponsors year after year, and more often than not, Ben dips into his own resources.

Belinda pursued the idea of portraits of herself and Ben, and in December 1994 I went to stay with them at Ashurst Wood. I can honestly say that none of my previous remarks about staying with people applied in this case. I felt completely at home and right in the heart of the cricket world. I could not have asked for more. Fortunately, they were pleased with their portraits, although I did have to make a slight alteration to Ben. They have been friends ever since and very supportive.

An article on my painting life appeared in *The Cricketer International* in 1995, which Peter Perchard, the sub-editor at the time, had asked me to write. He produced a whole series of the cricket grounds I had painted and over the years the magazine has continued to publish articles and illustrations. In 1999, I wrote at length about my Australian trip, which produced a flood of orders for prints. I also advertise my prints through *The Cricketer* each month as well as *Wisden*

Cricket Monthly. Advertising regularly and becoming well-known inevitably means a steady flow of requests for donations – mostly from cricket clubs – but also from larger charities. I always try to support them as much as possible. I donated an original painting to the Lady Taverners to be auctioned, which was bought by Leslie Thomas, and since then I have endeavoured to satisfy as many requests as possible. The Lord's Taverners, a great cricket charity, helps to promote cricket for the young as well as helping the disabled. The Lady Taverners, started ten years ago, raise an enormous amount of money for the disabled, as well as cricket in general.

The Brian Johnston Memorial Trust is a favourite of mine, and was set up by the family after Brian died in 1994 to give scholarships to children who could not afford to continue with cricket coaching or pursue a career in cricket. It also helps the blind – even to the extent of blind cricket for children.

It is a tragedy that there is no cricket in the daily curriculum of state schools and children do not readily have the opportunity to discover the game and play it. In Australia, they cannot believe that we have no cricket in our state schools and no competitive sport. These charities do an enormous amount of good in supporting and encouraging children and adults on their way to taking up the game professionally.

In 1995 I painted that loveliest of grounds in Hampshire – Warnford – owned by the Hampshire Hogs. One of their stalwart players is Christopher Bazalgette, not the youngest member of the side, but who, nevertheless, continues to take forty wickets per season. Christopher is the Advertisement Manager of *The Cricketer International*, a position he has held for twenty-six years. Whenever I need information, no matter in whatever part of the world, he is always on hand to supply the answers. He writes very informative articles on a wide range of subjects for *The Cricketer* and is one of the game's greatest characters. My painting of the Hampshire Hogs was bought by Rex Chester, a past President of this famous Club.

By 1997 I had been producing limited edition prints for twelve years in a very small way, and they were now starting to go well, though I was unable to market them as I should. I did not have enough time myself and could not find a suitable agent.

My very first limited edition prints were made in 1985 for the Royal Green Jackets' Centenary Match against I Zingari at St Cross, and the Royal Green Jackets also bought the original. I then painted IZ at Winchester College. This painting was bought by the Thorneycrofts, whose boys were in the First XI, from which they made prints. A painting of Meads, the lovely ground at Winchester College, followed. It is one of my favourite grounds and has a beautiful old wall round it. I consider it to be one of my best cricket paintings. I made a print out of it for the College – the Old Wykehamists' Society bought both the original and the limited edition.

I myself, made prints of the 1991 paintings of Lord's and Upper Club at Eton and Charterhouse School. I sold the prints to Gerald Bristowe, who had bought the original of Charterhouse. I eventually made other limited editions of Burton Court, the Lords and Commons at The Oval (the pavilion had not been refurbished then), and also a second painting of Paul Getty's ground. Schools take a limited edition and sell it to raise funds. The same applies to golf clubs.

About a year and a half ago I asked my sister-in-law, a former overseas sales representative of Hallmark Cards, to market prints with me. There seemed to be very little competition, and as I have become more widely known, the prints are selling well. It is very gratifying when people like Dean Headley, who took part in that electrifying match in Melbourne, think highly of them. A professional cricketer will know whether the game is portrayed correctly or not, and it is very pleasing to be complimented by the players themselves. People ring up from all over the world, at all times of the day or night, wanting prints of this or that match, and while they are about it, setting cricket matters to rights. I just wish the English selectors could hear them. I have never had a cross word with any of them, and find the cricket public in general very easy to get on with and extremely knowledgeable.

My prints are now marketed among other places through the county ground shops, but it is a pity that the art side is not more energetically promoted. I receive complaints all the time from members that there is a dearth of quality items in the art line in the county ground shops. Cricket and art have gone hand in hand from the very beginning, and if it were not for paintings and drawings, we would have no pictorial record of the game. Although largely superseded by the camera, there is still a place for the cricket artist in the scheme of things.

¹ Subsequently published in *The History of I Zingari*, R. L. Arrowsmith and B. J. W. Hill. 1982

Chapter 5 Cricket Takes Over

When I first started painting cricket in the eighties, I came as something of a surprise to people not used to seeing a woman out of context. At the Summerfields School v Cheam match, the master in charge came over to me and quizzed me on where my field placings were going to be. How could I possibly know anything about cricket, and how could I paint the subject without having any idea of how the field is set and how the game unfolds? I told him that I knew a great deal about cricket and that if he waited to the end, he would see that my field placings were correct. He came over later, looked at my painting, and was silent, which I suppose was a compliment.

I never encounter that sort of prejudice now. Perhaps I am more in command of my *métier,* and can speak informatively on the subject of cricket, so that nobody questions whether I know what I am doing or not. I sometimes receive kindly suggestions and advice which I never resent, but the animosity towards me as a woman painting cricket has disappeared. Women have a higher profile in the cricket world of the late nineties and the men seem to have resigned themselves to this feminine incursion. The West Indian cricket commentator, Donna Symmonds, has broken new ground with her Test Match Special commentaries, and of course, women are now eligible to be members of the MCC.

In 1992 Sir William Becher wrote to me saying that Sir Paul Getty was making his own ground at Wormsley and it was going to be opened that summer. I Zingari were going to play there in June and would it not be a lovely ground to paint? I contacted Paul Getty's office and they gave me permission to paint Wormsley, and to spend quite a lot of time there during the summer, as I had to complete the painting

At my easel

over several matches. The ground is rather like Arundel, in an amphitheatre. There were problems with the pitch in the early years and it had to be dug up and re-laid. Paul Getty holds a match there every fortnight, with a marquee, and it is very much centred around the lunch and the champagne. He invites well-known players to play for him and teams to play against him, and receives many applications from teams and players longing for an

invitation. Brian Johnston loved this ground and ran the cricket there until he died. It is in a magnificent setting and must have matured a great deal by now. I did two paintings of it, one in 1992, which Paul Getty bought, and the second in 1993 which I donated to the Princess of Wales Memorial Trust and the Lord's Taverners.

I always remember the ice cream man at Wormsley, who comes with his barrow and striped umbrella. The ices are homemade and given free to everybody who comes and watches. This is a nice gesture which is much appreciated, particularly by me, as ice cream is one of my passions. Tita used to tell of the time she took me to the Theatre Royal in Plymouth as a child to watch the ballet. First, I cast round anxiously to see if they had Wall's ice cream there. I remained completely impassive, giving no sign of life during the performance, but when the curtain fell for the first interval I clapped and clapped, bouncing up and down in my seat. My aunt thought she had made a breakthrough in my education but her hopes were dashed when I turned to her and said, beaming, 'It's Wall's, it's Wall's ...'

One of the matches I most enjoyed was during the Canterbury Festival week, a great occasion in Kent cricket. Kent played Worcestershire in perfect weather. I arrived the day before, was shown round and bagged my spot, where I was assured there would be nobody in front of me. It

Canterbury Festival Week

pastel

was a lovely position. I worked on it for five to six hours and came back the next day for the first day of the week, to find the whole area in front of me, albeit on a lower level, covered in cars. I was shattered. I had to move, which altered the angle so completely that I had to make a new start.

Two chaps from television, seeing that I was dug in for the day, asked if they could leave their equipment with me while they wandered round, to which I agreed. It so happened that one of them was Andy Steggall, sports presenter for GMTV and Meridian TV, based at Southampton. They were making a programme on county cricket in three counties – Kent, Hampshire and Sussex. Sussex would not take part, but the other two did. Matthew Fleming was their liaison at Kent, and they had left him with a video camera which he

HRH The Princess Royal   *pastel 1995*

used to do two or three interviews with me and also a great deal of filming. Andy Steggall mentioned that he would like to do a film on The Oval painting. He is a charming man and passionate about cricket. It is lovely to find a sports presenter who is really keen and modest to

boot. The painting turned out very well, I am happy to say. Graham Cowdrey bought most of the subsequent limited edition prints for his Benefit Year and Matthew Fleming bought the original off the easel. Kent is a leading cricketing county, with a great tradition, headed by

E. W. Swanton, who lives at Sandwich.

The Royal Corinthian Yacht Club wanted a portrait of their patron HRH The Princess Royal. Pat Dyas, the Admiral, asked me if I would be interested in this commission. I readily confirmed that I would, whereupon he broached the subject with the Princess, assuring her that it would be informal and in sailing gear. Princess Anne agreed. There were to be two sittings only, of one hour each, to take place in the Yellow Drawing Room at Buckingham Palace. Pat Dyas wanted to be present as he knew the Princess well and thought she might be more relaxed if he was there. Six months elapsed before I suddenly found myself driving into Buckingham Palace court-yard for my first sitting.

I was astonished to find that Princess Anne is far better looking than her photographs would suggest. Her skin is magnificent and her intelligent, deep blue eyes light up her face. She was a conscientious sitter, never altering her position while keeping up an animated conversation with both of us. I was allowed to take some photographs as the two sittings

England v West Indies, Trent Bridge, 1995

pastel

were short and was very pleased that, at the next appointment, she offered me a third sitting, sensing that I would need it.

The completed portrait, which Princess Anne never saw, was well received by the officers and members of the Royal Corinthian Yacht Club at Cowes, and now hangs in the main entrance. On taking a quick look before it was finished, the Princess announced that I had flattered her, but this was how I saw her.

The summer of 1995 saw me painting a Test Match at Edgbaston of England v the West Indies. England collapsed after two days, leaving me to complete the painting with no crowd and no players, but I could see what was going to happen and got in the essentials early. I had excellent television coverage, and was amused to find that I was beginning to be recognised, particularly in my favourite Indian restaurant. I then painted the West Indies at Trent Bridge (a drawn game) in wonderful weather. The television coverage was again quite excellent from my point of view, doing me a great deal of good.

My mother's eightieth birthday was marked by an exhibition at the Ebury Galleries in Ebury Street in October 1995. The Galleries, run by John Adams, are an ideal venue and turned out to be an excellent choice. My mother had painted solidly all that summer at my house on the Isle of Wight, while I rushed from one cricket match to another. The exhibition was a pleasing success and she sold three-

Tita on a visit to Glyndebourne

quarters of her stock – not bad for an eighty-year-old.

Later in the year, my beloved Tita had been taken seriously ill and I insisted on staying with her in the hospital near Salisbury. Since I had lost my driving licence for three months (not through drink, I hasten to add), I was effectively marooned and spent my days seeing to her needs, chivvying the nursing staff who chopped and changed without reference to previous instructions, while trying to keep cheerful under the strain. Painting was temporarily abandoned and for once I had time for contemplation. However, it did not take long for Tita to succumb and after the initial shock, life slowly returned to normal.

Tita had been a huge influence and left an enormous gap in my life. She had been a second mother to me, a tiny indomitable woman with kindly blue eyes who saw only good in everybody and who, right up to the age of ninety-three, busied herself in her garden. Her one thought was for other people. She had no money to speak

of, yet always gave to everyone who came knocking at her door. She was a devout Catholic but did not always approve of every innovation ordered by the Vatican. She could not bear the 'sign of peace' when she had to turn to her neighbours and shake their hand. When the priest descended on her during mass and shook her hand, offering her the sign of peace, she would say 'How do you do?' which made him laugh. She had been a friend of Siegfried Sassoon who was also captivated by her wit and energy. I learnt much from Tita and will always be grateful for the sensible, loving and simple way in which she tried to guide me.

The year 1996 was very trying for me but I completed cricket paintings of Epsom College and Elstree School near Newbury. The latter commission came about through Lord Bramall who had bumped into me on many occasions painting I Zingari or the Royal Green Jackets. At first they wanted just the school to be in the painting but I persuaded them to have the junior cricket in the foreground with the house in the background. It was to be presented to the master, who had run the cricket for many years, on his retirement. It turned out to be one of my best efforts and he was thrilled to be given this well-kept secret.

Towards the end of that summer I trailed up to Hagley Hall, owned by Lord Cobham whose father was Governor of IZ. The I Zingari match is a long-standing

Elstree School   *pastel*

Epsom College   *pastel*

I Zingari at Hagley Hall

pastel

England v Pakistan, The Oval, 1996

pastel

Redvers Parker   *pastel*

Stroma Parker   *pastel*

England v Australia, Old Trafford, 1997

pastel

Cheltenham Cricket Festival, 1997   *pastel*

Jocelyn Galsworthy

South of France   *pastel*
View from Stephen and Carole Lee's villa
near Saint-Raphael.

Bayeux, Normandy   *pastel*

La Petite Chapelle du Verger, Cancale   *pastel*

fixture, although nowadays it has been curtailed to one day instead of two. Hagley is a beautiful ground with the church behind the pavilion overlooked by the Hall with its sloping lawns. The cricket field is surrounded by the estate and the deer graze right up to the boundary – just the setting for a special painting.

The rest of that summer was taken up with the Canterbury Festival, England v Pakistan at The Oval and a series of seascapes in the Isle of Wight.

The following year was extremely strenuous. I always continue to paint in the winter, long after the cricket season is over, and do most of my portraits at this time. As summer approached, I had fixtures at Old Trafford, Headingley, the Cheltenham Cricket Festival and various smaller matches. In addition, my mother and I held a small joint exhibition on the Isle of Wight, at the Bembridge Gallery, in between my cricket appointments.

At Old Trafford (Australia v England), Henry Blofeld did me proud on Test Match Special. I even got a call from Michael Shatin, a prominent barrister from Melbourne, in the middle of the night to say he was watching me on television. It was the first time I had encountered the public at close quarters during a Test Match. I was crammed into the back of the VIP box, and had the parents and friends of the Australian team in front of me. They were all very complimentary about my work, and Steve Waugh's parents asked if

they could have first refusal, which I was happy to give them. However, due to a misunderstanding, they did not take it up in time. The painting was snapped up by John Hartley, an aficionado of the game, whom I included in the picture while he was watching. By this time, I had been at Old Trafford for seven days, rooted to the spot for almost twelve hours a day. A member of the public brushed past and seriously asked me how many paintings of the Test Match I did a day! I was lost for words. This third Test Match levelled the Series for Australia, the Lord's Test having been washed out. Steve Waugh batted on with a damaged hand and made a century in both innings, while England let the game slip completely. It was Dean Headley's debut in Test cricket, and he told me recently with a wry smile that those two centuries were made off his bowling, a fact he will never forget.

At Headingley, the weather was appalling and the BBC wanted to take the spot I had been allocated. I would have none of it and stood my ground when confronted by the head of the BBC Outside Broadcast Unit. Together with the thunderstorms and the level of cricket, it was not a happy Test. All my work of that season, with the exception of those paintings bought off the easel, went into my exhibition at the Ebury Galleries in October 1997.

The exhibition was opened by Sir Nicholas Scott, whose portrait I had done

when he was a young MP in the sixties. He is an ardent cricketer and regularly plays for the Lords and Commons which is how I met him again after many years. The exhibition went off to a flying start and was my most financially rewarding to date. Pauline Johnston spoke very convincingly on behalf of the Brian Johnston Memorial Trust which was to benefit from the proceeds. I shall always remember my devoted mother, seated at a table, as glamorous as ever, making sure everyone signed the visitors' book. She had offered to do this important task and, deaf as she was, managed to catch everyone. Little did I know it would be her last social trip to London. The gallery was packed, bursting at the seams and my brother and sister-in-law could hardly cope on the sales desk. I showed a variety of subjects – portraits, cricket scenes, landscapes, seascapes, and pen and ink sketches – hoping there would be something for everyone. Thankfully, sales were outstanding and commissions were booked months ahead.

There is a price to pay for everything, and my mother, now eighty-two, was not well. Eventually, she was diagnosed with leukaemia with the prognosis of two to three years left to live. She started painting for another exhibition, despite having to endure blood transfusions every three weeks. She was stoic in the extreme and remarkably unafraid. I meantime, had organised to go to the West Indies in

England v Australia, Headingley, 1997

pastel

The late Emma Grace   *pastel*

March of the following year to paint the Test Matches, and my mother insisted I stick to the plan.

I had never been to the Caribbean before and, full of excitement, flew to Barbados. This feeling soon vanished as the hotel, not used to guests getting up at crack of dawn and disappearing to do a day's work, refused to give me breakfast, so I did without. That was unpleasant enough, but then I became dehydrated as well, because I simply did not drink enough, and went down with a kidney ailment. However, the cricket was fantastic and the atmosphere quite unforgettable.

When I arrived with Trevor Bailey at the Kensington Oval, two days before the start of the match, there was chaos, and a complete lack of organisation. It was a building site and the Test Match Special team had been given a box with only a partial view of the ground. The same thing applied to Sky Television. The team from Test Match Special had to move to their old box over the Pickwick Pavilion below which I was sitting. The very enjoyable Test Match was ruined on the last day by Old Trafford weather, but the camaraderie was wonderful. I was situated next to the West Indian dressing rooms in the area of the England players' wives, the scorers' table and umpires' room. There was plenty of chatter and plenty of interruption.

I remember Rory Bremner coming to the Pickwick Pavilion with Matthew Fleming who introduced me. Rory suddenly saw Henry Blofeld walking back to the West Indian commentary box across the ground and at once started imitating his plummy tones. Everyone hooted with laughter. Matthew Fleming was asked for his pass, and pointed out mildly that he was with the England team. The steward looked blank and refused to believe him. After the usual arguments, he was reluctantly allowed to stay.

We then flew to Antigua, not perhaps the prettiest island, and the so-called four star hotel reminded me of Spain in the fifties where nothing worked, the difference being that in Spain, in those days, the prices were very low. I had plenty to say, and fell out with all the staff all the time. They simply could not understand that, to me, time was of the essence and that when I said I needed something at a certain time, I meant it. If I had merely been on holiday, it would not have mattered so much.

My first encounter with the Chief Executive of the cricket ground did not

The Sovereign's Parade, Royal Military Academy, Sandhurst   *pastel*

Pétanque aux Remparts, St Malo
pen & ink drawing

Boules à la Porte de Dinan, St Malo
pen & ink drawing

L'Après-Midi à la Plage du Mole, St Malo
pen & ink drawing

'La Tricoteuse'
pen & ink drawing

England v West Indies, Kensington Oval, Barbados, 1998   *pastel*

Jocelyn Galsworthy

England v West Indies, St John's Recreation Ground – Antigua. 1988

pastel

Beach scene, Barbados

pastel

Beach scene, Antigua featuring Trevor Bailey's yellow T-shirt, 1998

pastel

bode well for our future relationship. He had made an appointment to meet me at 2.30 p.m. and eventually turned up two hours late. The secretaries and officials merely laughed at my discomfiture. He proposed the most unsuitable spot from which to paint, which I declined and after much heated discussion, I was eventually given a cordoned-off space in the disabled area which was fine. To me, the attitude of all the officials seemed very aggressive and left a bad impression, so I guessed I had much to learn about the way things are done in the West Indies. On the other hand, the cricket was something one will never experience anywhere else. The local character, Gravy, was in full flight, spectators hung from every tree around the ground while steel bands with their inimitable sound kept up a ceaseless throbbing, except at the crucial moments of the game when they fell silent. While I was painting, a West Indian supporter in the adjacent Andy Roberts stand continuously shouted 'Watch de ball, man' to every delivery of the West Indian innings that day. I shouted across to him 'I wish you'd give that advice to the English'. Everyone laughed but, unperturbed, he continued his relentless chanting much to everyone's amusement. Apart from the collapse of English cricket, it was a great Test Match to experience. From an artist's point of view, it was paradise.

The weather let us down with heavy rain and only sponges to mop up the ground. Their 'whale' (a huge mechanical roller with sponges to soak up the water) had gone up in a puff of smoke after the first ten minutes of use. I was desperate to preserve my painting from the water, and the staff who were brushing the excess away in all directions, soaking everybody. Luckily, I whisked my painting away under cover before the West Indies won the game and the Series, because the area which had comfortably held twenty people was invaded by a hundred; I was pinned to the wall, clinging on to my possessions, while women holding babies and munching chicken legs swarmed all around. My finished painting was bought by a local barrister, supposedly one of Antigua's millionaires. He had been born in St John, baptised in the church across the way from the ground, and knew everyone on the Board.

As well as my cricket paintings, I did a seascape of the beach at Halcyon Cove, Antigua and one in Barbados. The former, featuring Trevor Bailey in his yellow T-shirt, was bought on the beach by Bob Bevan, a prominent Lord's Taverner.

On my return to London, my mother told me she had been thrilled to see me on television. Henry Blofeld again mentioned me on Test Match Special so I had fair coverage.

My mother continued with her flower paintings, turning out some beautiful pictures – remarkable under the circumstances. Between my brother, his wife and myself we managed to look after her in her home at Swanage, but it was a great strain and I do not know how I managed to paint. But paint I did: the Tunbridge Wells Cricket Festival, Trent Bridge Test, Memorial Match at Lord's for The Princess of Wales, Hampshire and Sussex county grounds, Cricketer Cup Final, a private ground in Kent for John Sunley and the Bunbury XI v The President's XI at Chobham Cricket Club, commissioned by Edward Bentall.

Just as I was completing my painting of the Cricketer Cup Final, I received a telephone call and rushed down to Swanage in the middle of the night. I spent two weeks in hospital with my mother who knew she would never come out. When she died, in circumstances of great dignity and with unfailing optimism that she would soon be in a better place, it was a terrible blow to me and my brother. She was my favourite companion, so much fun to be with and much more like a sister than a mother.

It was her last wish that I should go ahead with an exhibition of her paintings. This was her legacy to me, and part of the proceeds were to go in gratitude to the hospital where she ended her life. She was so pleased that I would be going to Australia, and she was able to discuss my plans with me while she was dying in her characteristically unselfish way.

Happily, all the preparations I had made before setting off on my Australian

Jocelyn Galsworthy

trip came to fruition. On arrival at Adelaide (without the slightest effect from jet-lag), I telephoned Terry Davies at The Oval and went to see him that afternoon. He was as nice in person as he had been on the telephone, and showed me round, providing me with a fantastic position in the lower press box.

I started the initial sketch that afternoon, and began in earnest the next morning, so that I had a day or so before the Test to put in the background. I dragged all my painting gear up two flights of stairs, noticing the heat, but not minding it. So long as it did not rain, I would be happy. On the morning of the Test Match I found myself next to Chris Lander (cricket correspondent for the *Daily Mirror*), with Derek Pringle in front of me. If they were somewhat surprised to have next to them an untidy artist, with all her belongings stuffed into every possible corner, they certainly did not show it. I was thrilled to have cricket writers around me and to be able to discuss, while painting, the lamentable English performance. I had never really mixed with journalists before and was struck by their obvious concern and frustration at what they were witnessing. Chris kept me supplied with water all day long, afraid that I would become dehydrated. Stephen Fay, a Wagner buff (the Ring Cycle was on at the Adelaide Opera House), sat a few steps lower down, and the rowdy corporate boxes were behind me. Luckily, things

grew quieter as they watched me painting, and when we struck up a conversation, not a single oath was to be heard. They were hilariously funny with their advice to the Poms, sadly all too true. It was a treat to find the corporate boxes so interested in the cricket, instead of watching football on television and drinking non-stop as they do at home. They never missed a ball and were keen to be included in my painting. The temperature was by now 42°C but one of them rushed to a spot in front of me, standing immobile for forty-five minutes, for the honour of being included in the picture. He then gave me a bottle of champagne for my trouble.

The Adelaide Oval is an extremely pretty ground, with the cathedral opposite the pavilion, grassy slopes where the public may sit at will, and tented over with colourful awnings. It was a shame that England put on such a pitiful performance. Alec Stewart lost the toss and, on one of the very hottest days, England had to field all day. This, of course, was bad luck. The match ended at lunch time on the fifth day. I had another three days in Adelaide so I took the tram to the beach and went for a swim. The next day, I titivated the painting and took the finished article to show Terry Davies and his Chief Executive at the Adelaide Oval. They were full of compliments and wondered how I had managed to cope with the extreme heat while producing a picture which, they said, conveyed the

atmosphere so well.

As I had time to spare before the next Test in Melbourne, I decided to take the train which, with hindsight, proved to be a mistake. The rest of the group had gone sight-seeing to Ayers Rock or had flown to Tasmania, but I could not cart all my heavy painting paraphernalia about. A brief word to the uninitiated about the Australian railway system – make sure you travel light. They informed me at the ticket office that my luggage would not fit into my compartment, and they were right. The first-class sleeper was tiny, even with everything folded away. At night, when the bed was lowered, there was no room to stand. I had to strap my portfolios containing my precious completed picture, my paper and my boards to the slatted shelf behind the door, which was too high for me to reach. My hand luggage had to be squeezed in where possible. Fortunately, I met a charming woman from Sussex on the platform, who suggested we have dinner together. There was, however, no restaurant car on the nine-hour journey, so we bought a bottle of wine and sat in her compartment, companionably drowning our sorrows. I then remained sitting up all night in my compartment, as there was no room for the bed. Breakfast never appeared, and when I went in search of it, I found a cross man in a cubby-hole trying to prepare the trays. It was all so unappetising when it finally arrived, that I went hungry.

Tunbridge Wells Cricket Festival, 1998

pastel

Jocelyn Galsworthy

Hampshire County Cricket Club, County Ground, Southampton, 1998

pastel

Cricket at Godmersham, 1998   *pastel*

Diana, Princess of Wales Memorial Match, Lord's, 1998 *pastel*

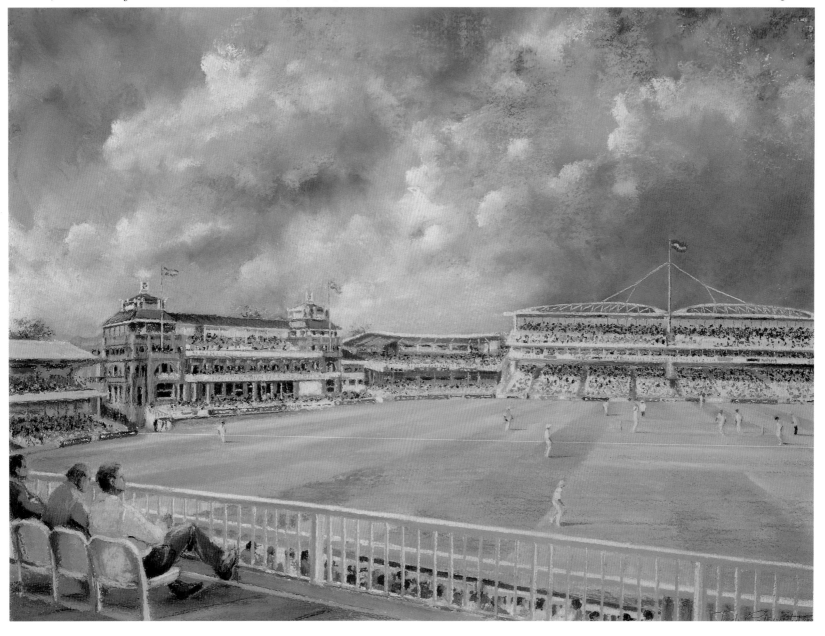

Sussex County Cricket Club, County Ground, Hove, 1998

pastel

England v Australia, Adelaide Oval, 1998

The last two hours of the journey to Melbourne showed a barren, scorched landscape with the odd eucalyptus tree. A friendly Australian girl alerted me to the fact that we were coming in to Melbourne station and assisted me with my luggage, as the conductor was far from helpful. As at Adelaide, there were no trolleys or porters. By this time I was furious and, grabbing a heavy, flat-bed trolley with a wire cage on top (normally pulled by a machine), I pushed it towards the luggage van which held my large suitcase. As with a wilful supermarket trolley, it had a mind of its own, and I nearly ended up on a collision course with the engine. The Australian girl and I piled it with our luggage and headed for the taxi rank. An irate shout went up from the controller and I thought we were going to be arrested. A shouting match ensued, until my Australian friend told him that this was no way to behave to a visitor. He calmed down and even escorted me and my luggage to a taxi.

In Melbourne for the fourth Test, my accommodation came as a shock after the lovely room I had been given in Adelaide. I moved several times, finally settling into a room with a large terrace. I loathe air conditioning and sealed windows. Surprisingly, the city was completely dead, even though Christmas was just around the corner.

I was very pleased to hear Michael Shatin on the telephone, immediately on arrival at the hotel, telling me that he was going to take me to a Club match on the outskirts of Melbourne that afternoon. This was an enlightening experience – District Grade Cricket is of an exceptionally high standard and I could see at once that the quality of our County Cricket could in no way match it. Prahran was playing South Melbourne. Both these sides have an illustrious list of former and present players, for example Julian Wiener, Sam Loxton, John Emburey, Aravinda da Silva, Derek Randall, Lindsey Hassett, Keith Miller, Damien Fleming, Dave Watmore and Asanka Gurusinha. However, it is interesting to note that Prahran, although playing superb cricket, is only fourteenth in the League Table.

This match was one of the most exciting draws I have ever watched, with both sides batting, bowling and fielding superbly. It is worth remembering that Australian cricketers, except for approximately an elite twenty-two, are not contracted to their clubs or states and have full-time jobs. If they play for their state, they are paid by the day and allowed time off by their employers. This encourages a highly competitive system from which emerges a top class Test side. I cannot understand why we do not introduce something similar into the way we organise cricket at our County level.

Throughout the afternoon at Prahran Club I sat with Bob Parish, former Chief Executive of the Australian Cricket Board. This delightful man enlightened me as to the reasons for introducing One Day cricket, coloured clothing and Day/Night matches on to the international scene. He was in no doubt that such measures have been good for the standards of cricket and crowd participation. After the recent World Cup in England, I agree that the standard of cricket was superb, but I still think that an uneven One Day match is the most boring element of modern cricket. The fluctuations in a Test Match, however drawn out, can dramatically change the outcome of the match, and bring excitement right up to the last over. I was very glad to have witnessed the high standards of this level of Club cricket in Australia which sits just below the Sheffield Shield Competition.

On Monday, I set off for the Melbourne Cricket Ground to be shown round by Michelle Harding, who had been delegated to look after me by Peter French, the Acting Secretary. It is a marvellously impressive ground dominated by the great southern stand. It was difficult to decide which side of the ground to paint, and difficult too, to find somewhere where people would not encircle me. I found a spot outside the press box in the Extra Members' Section. Michelle offered to take out the seating if I did not have enough room. This was done and I put my easel in place, well pleased with such a fabulous position. I was all set to begin painting next morning, giving me plenty of time before the start of the match on Boxing Day. The ground itself is really a football stadium (Aussie Rules) but when full with a cricket crowd, has an electric atmosphere.

On Christmas Eve, I went to Midnight Mass in St Patrick's Cathedral in Melbourne. I arrived one-and-a-half hours early and it was already filling up. Five thousand people crammed themselves into a space meant to hold one thousand. The music was simply superb, and you could have heard a pin drop throughout the service. I have never experienced the like. On the way out, I introduced myself to the Archbishop of Melbourne, complimented him on the service and explained my reason for being in Australia. He knew how the English team was struggling and suggested they might need our prayers. The Almighty must have been listening as the Melbourne Test was a triumph for England.

I spent Christmas Day away from my easel, with Michael Shatin and his family, who entertained me royally. His eldest son, aged six, and I played cricket on the lawn – a good way to shake down one's Christmas lunch. Michael was a member of the Melbourne Cricket Club who have a very close relationship with our MCC at Lord's and pride themselves on their reciprocal arrangements.

The first day of the Test was on Saturday, Boxing Day, and I set off early from my hotel to put all my painting equipment in place. As usual, the Australian security people were very helpful. I fastened down all the loose bits by tying them to the seats, stowed my precious things with security, and walked across the park for breakfast with the Lord's Taverners. The marvellous Michael Shatin had arranged for me to be a guest at the traditional breakfast which takes place every Boxing Day before the Test Match in Melbourne. It was a magnificent occasion. Trevor Bailey and his wife Greta were very surprised to see me, and I met many friends and acquaintances from England. Trevor gave an amusing speech, as did Tony Lewis, now President of the MCC. My neighbour at table, Donald Rich, former Chairman of Hampshire County Cricket Club, and I decided, as time was running on, to slip out unobtrusively and make our way back to the ground. I walked back across the park in an unexpected drizzle which never let up. It was most depressing, though not cold, and must have infuriated the authorities who had worked so hard for their great social occasion of the year. The rain worsened steadily. Peter Baxter's Radio 5 link, in the form of a cable right over my head which dipped just above my painting, caused the rainwater to drip down and sent me rushing for my portfolio with which to cover my painting. I remained glued to my spot until just after 5 p.m. when the game was called off. This period of boredom was alleviated by long conversations and cricket discussions with Michael Henderson, then writing for *The Times* but now cricket correspondent for *The Daily Telegraph*. I at once found someone of like mind, not afraid to say what he thinks. A great music buff, he also found the time to write the programme notes for the Ring Cycle at the Adelaide Opera House.

The temperature on Christmas Day had been 43°C. By the Sunday of the Melbourne Test it had plummeted to 11°C with a bitter wind coming directly from the Antarctic. I had not thought to bring my usual layers of wool and so had to buy two extra jerseys from the MCC shop. However, it was fine and intermittently sunny, and the public flocked to the ground in their thousands undeterred by the intense cold. A full house at the MCG is quite an experience.

Monday dawned brighter and warmer, with a great day's cricket in prospect. They started earlier in the morning to make up for the time lost on Saturday due to the weather. On Tuesday, play again began at 10.30 in the morning. It was one of those days hard to repeat, with the game swinging from one side to the other. Steve Waugh made a brilliant century but Darren Gough and Dean Headley, backed up by superb fielding, demolished the rest. Play continued until after 7.30 p.m., one of the longest days ever recorded in Test Match history, and England won. The shadows were deep across the playing area and there was some confusion as to whether the last overs would be played the next morning. The Australians around me had all gone home at lunchtime, thinking that the outcome was a foregone conclusion. They must have had a terrible shock when they turned on their radios and televisions that evening to find that the reverse was true. The Australians who remained were stunned into silence. The barmy army swept across the ground, having been in full voice all day. From a distance, they had behaved well and had been fun, giving England the support they needed. We all felt elated to have won that Test, not least because it would give some life to the end of the Series at Sydney. There was quite a party back at the hotel, where the team was also staying.

New Year's Eve saw me flying to Sydney – a fantastic city. It is very beautiful because of the harbour, and by some miracle has not been spoilt. The cosmopolitan and multi-cultural mix was right up my street, with gourmet food and wines, discreet, efficient service and everyone very kind and, seemingly, unmercenary. As it was New Year's Eve, the streets were packed with exuberant people gathering to watch the fireworks, and I do not think I have ever been caught up in such a good-humoured mass of young people, drinking, dancing and swirling round me. I was frightened of losing my companions, but we held on tight and eventually reached our hotel. The whole evening was an unforgettable introduction to Sydney.

I was greatly relieved to be able to paint on New Year's Day and to choose a spot on the level of the Don Bradman stand, not in the members' area but where things are usually quiet, just below the televison and radio commentary boxes. I had a good view of the pavilion and ladies' pavilion on the right and the large new stand straight ahead. For the four days of the Sydney Test, the marvellous security people came to collect me and all my baggage and put me in a taxi back to my hotel at the end of each day. They carried my paraphernalia up three floors to my pitch every single day and I could not thank them enough.

As the final Test got under way, Alec Stewart looked settled and was set for a big score. Sadly, as so often happens, he threw away his wicket as did Mark Butcher, and the game changed dramatically. All the progress England had made in Melbourne seemed to slip away and the match was a total anti-climax after Darren Gough's superb bowling and hat trick. The match had drawn one of the biggest crowds Sydney had seen for a Test Match for many years and it was only a pity that England failed to rise to the occasion.

On my last day in Sydney, I had lunch at an excellent restaurant on Darling Harbour, before making my way to the airport for the long flight home. I had promised to be at the wedding of one of my young friends the next day.

I feel I must mention Qantas and the VIP treatment they gave me, coming and going as well as on their internal flight between Melbourne and Sydney. The Flight Director, the very man who had been so kind at Heathrow on the outward journey, met me at Sydney Airport and once again set things in motion, so that my precious painting materials were well looked after, and I had the minimum to carry myself. They even gave me two bottles of Krug. I promised to send all the Flight Directors a print, as they are all cricket mad. Australia had been quite an experience and one which I would happily repeat.

Jocelyn Galsworthy

England v Australia, MCG, Melbourne, 1998. The Longest Day's Play in Test Cricket

pastel

England v Australia, SCG, Sydney, 1999. 'Darren Gough's Hat-Trick'   *pastel*

Chapter 6   Carnival of Cricket

On returning to England, there was little time to spare before the World Cup. I also had The Oval painting to work on and needed to make progress with that before the start of the 1999 season. Although the books were supposed to be closed for any further applicants in August 1998, things had drifted on and I felt obliged to accept any late arrivals.

Arrangements to paint the World Cup at Lord's, Edgbaston, Worcester and Taunton were fraught with difficulties because of the position with the English Cricket Board who had sold the copyright to any reproductions. If I had not been very determined, I would have given up. In the end, there was no copyright problem and the ECB provided the necessary space at Edgbaston, but Worcester and Taunton issued passes for me themselves. As for Lord's, I prevailed on the good nature of British Airways who have Box 22 in the new grandstand. Karen Marshall, MCC Marketing Director, asked them on my behalf whether I could paint the opening match – England v Sri Lanka on 14th May.

I arrived at Lord's by taxi with all my paraphernalia early in the morning and dragged it up to the box. I set myself up and started to paint. The weather was unsettled but the ground was humming and full of expectation. The box gradually filled and John Morgan, who was host, at once made me feel welcome. Tracey Galsworthy, my sister-in-law, was at the Tours Office at the Grace Gates, taking orders for our prints. The Prime Minister spoke a few words to open the tournament (it is a pity that the loudspeaker system failed for part of it) and the Carnival of Cricket was under way.

Sri Lanka did not perform to their potential and it was a comfortable win for England. I had only achieved the basics of this painting in the time but it had the makings of something special with the new NatWest Media Centre at the fore of the composition. I asked BA if I could return for the Super Six Match on 9th June. They were enthusiastic and did not seem perturbed by the disruption to their box.

I set off for Worcester at 5.30 a.m. on Sunday 16th May for the Australia v Scotland match. I have never been amongst so many Scots in England at one time, and what a party there was! Most of them had no idea about cricket but were good fun and, although completely 'tanked up', very well-behaved and unaggressive. The constant banter with the Australian spectators was good-humoured. Scotland played incredibly well and gave Australia a few hairy moments. I spent the whole week at Worcester, painting the background in order to put in the Sri Lanka v Zimbabwe match the following Saturday. The Worcester ground looked a picture, and the flaming red of Zimbabwe in the field, against the fabulous backdrop of the cathedral and trees, helped to create a stunning painting. Sri Lanka won all too easily, but their hopes were soon to be dashed.

On to Taunton for the next match in the World Cup Series. The interest in this match, Sri Lanka v India, was overwhelming. They came in their thousands and, although I was between the members' areas, the seats had been sold by the ECB to non-members. I had Indians on one side and Sri Lankans on the other. The steel band performed behind us and the Indian drums a few paces away. There were fire-crackers beside me and banners in front. The noise was deafening and the atmosphere electric. It was as if this sleepy, county ground had been transported to the West Indies or Calcutta and it worked – what a match. Dravid and Ganguly excelled themselves and records were broken all round. It did not seem to matter that India won so easily. The ground was packed to capacity, the armed forces kept brilliant order and the presence of police horses breathing down my neck before the close of play gave me the strangest sensation. My painting caused interest and comment and, when they were not all jumping up and down, they took the time to look and discuss.

I just managed to finish the painting before departing for Gloucester on a freezing, windy Sunday Bank Holiday. Planet 24, who make the programme Watercolour Challenge for Channel 4, had persuaded me to join two other

Sri Lanka v Zimbabwe, World Cup 1999, County Ground, Worcester　　　　　　　　*pastel*

India v Sri Lanka, World Cup 1999, County Ground, Taunton

pastel

professional artists to paint a watercolour on site and on camera for a Watercolour Challenge Special. We were to depict a charity match (in aid of Mark Alleyne's Benefit) between the Bunbury XI and Gloucestershire on Archdeacon Meadow, where they hold the Cricket Festival.

I agreed with some reservation. The last time I had used watercolours, I was in my teens. I also take my time, and am no good against the clock. Jack Russell, brilliant wicket keeper for Gloucestershire and England and now a successful artist, was to be the adjudicator. Hannah Gordon, the delightful presenter of the programme, welcomed us all warmly on a bitter day with a howling wind, leaden skies and no crowd. However, Geoffrey Jones, Rob Perry and myself did our best in the allotted time of four hours to capture the atmosphere and movement of the match, as well as the beauty of Archdeacon Meadow with Gloucester Cathedral in the background.

Our styles were very different. Geoffrey Jones is a prominent cartoonist and Rob Perry is a cricket artist specialising in portraits of cricketers. Samples of our work (in my case the Test in Antigua and a portrait of the late Brian Johnston) were shown, so that the television audience could be aware of what we could achieve when not under pressure. The men were far quicker than me, which I had expected, and the prize deservedly went to Rob Perry. The programme

appeared in August 1999 and, viewing it as a spectator, I felt reasonably content with what I had produced, given that a cricket match normally takes me six days to fully complete.

After twenty-four hours with friends in Cornwall, I returned to London. I was exhausted – nobody has any idea of the pressure there is in painting international cricket, especially in England. It entails hours of driving, lugging one's gear upstairs and downstairs, making sure nothing gets damaged, coping with the cold wind and the rain, setting up, taking down and, most important of all, achieving a high standard of work. Then there is the wonderful public – well-meaning but sometimes irritating. The sort of thing I have to put up with is neatly illustrated by an incident which happened when I was painting on the Duver at St Helen's in the Isle of Wight. A couple came along with their dogs and paused to examine what I was doing. They were enthusiastic and so were their dogs who, after a sniff round my sou'wester and jumper lying beside me, lifted their legs in unison and soaked them.

The day before, some children had been observing me painting a beach scene, and I heard one little chap say, 'Please Mummy, I want to give her a pound, but she hasn't got a hat'. I always knew I should have been a pavement artist.

However, I have established some

worthwhile contacts from many unexpected conversations and discussions on cricket. I wish the authorities would canvass the opinion of the devotees of the game amongst the general public. I myself am regularly approached by people who give vent to their frustration concerning English cricket. One recurring theme is that the gap between Test and County Cricket is immense, unlike Australia, where the Sheffield Shield competition is every bit as pressurised as the international scene.

Back in London I prepared for the Super Sixes at Lord's on 9th June, and started the Honourable Artillery Company's ground in the City of London, where Lloyds v The Stock Exchange were due to play a charity match in aid of the Brian Johnston Memorial Trust on 6th July. After England's exit from the World Cup at Edgbaston on 31st May, I decided that my painting of Lord's with the new Media Centre would feature Australia v Zimbabwe in the Super Sixes, rather than England's opening match against the holders of the trophy. The match was great fun for me, with Mark Nicholas (Channel 4 front-line commentator) and his party in the box on one side, and guests of the ECB on the other. I met our host, Ian Flower, for the first time, and although the match was somewhat flat with Australia dominating throughout, I had a captive audience and plenty of comments on my work. Mark Nicholas made

Cricket at Armoury House, the home of The Honourable Artillery Company

pastel

World Cup 1999 Semi-Final, Australia v South Africa, Edgbaston.
'The Greatest One Day International of All Time'.   *pastel*

Jocelyn Galsworthy

World Cup Final 1999, Lord's, Australia v Pakistan   *pastel*

some useful suggestions, which I acted on and the painting rapidly progressed. It was completed at a later date, when Lord's was peaceful and quiet.

I set off for Edgbaston very early on Sunday 13th June. Warwickshire had a League match against Lancashire that afternoon – the standard was so low that I could hardly bear to watch. I had been given a place, right on the boundary, an ideal spot from which to paint. I had a perfect view of the wicket and the quaint pavilion, which I am sure one day will be 'refurbished', and probably lose its character.

The semi-final arrived – Australia v South Africa. This must have been the greatest One Day International ever played. Australia batted first and set South Africa a reasonable score. The South African innings swung like a pendulum until they needed one run to win with three balls left. Klusener was on strike with Donald at the other end. Klusener struck the ball, called, charged down the wicket but Donald was rooted to the spot. Donald started to run, lost his bat and was run out by miles. It was a tragedy for the South Africans but one has to admire the Aussie tenacity. Can you imagine England in the same situation? Although the match was drawn, Australia won because of their position ahead of South Africa in the Super Six table. Everyone felt desperately sorry for South Africa, even the Australians, but this was world cricket at

the highest level and it was a pity there had to be a loser.

The final could never match the excitement and thrill of Edgbaston. Lord's was a picture – there is so much pride here and the developments have been so cleverly introduced, in fact, I think enhancing that glorious pavilion. The Pakistanis did their best outside the ground to liven up the atmosphere. Fireworks shot off in all directions but everything soon became very subdued as Australia completely ran away with the game, fielding first, and then reaching the batting target in the afternoon with hours and overs to spare. The public, who had paid a very high price for entry, were not amused. The Australian partying continued for hours, while I strove to progress with my painting in an empty Lord's.

I spent many days afterwards completing both the World Cup paintings. British Airways gave me full use of their box for as long as needed. Ian Flower, who runs the box, is a real cricket buff which is most unusual among the corporate crowd. Normally they are there for a day out entertaining clients, who might as well be at motor racing. I think this is detrimental to cricket in this country. So often, real cricket lovers are unable to acquire tickets and hundreds of seats remain empty while the business crowd prop up the bar and return to their seats for the last few overs. To add to this problem, County clubs are run for corporate benefit and

members frequently feel unwanted. I encounter this all over the country and the membership has a right to feel aggrieved. I cannot understand why parts of the Test ground are not kept for those members of the public who wish to buy tickets on the day at a reasonable price. Tickets for County matches should be half their present cost – surely teams would be far more encouraged by a packed ground than by a mere handful of spectators.

The idea of the World Cup as a tournament is inspired. It clearly demonstrates the value of the game in binding so many dissimilar peoples together. Remarkably, despite the political hostility between two nations of the sub-continent, there was no hint of it between the teams wherever they played, even when playing each other. On the whole, the respect the players have for each other, wherever they come from, is most gratifying and bears out what I have always thought about cricket, namely that it brings out the best in people.

I have always found painting at Lord's an enlightening experience. This great club strives to maintain high standards which is not easy in this sloppy age when the public often resents any form of discipline in dress and behaviour. The MCC have certain rules, but they are also relaxed, and bend over backwards to help. I always marvel at how the stewards, often devotees of the game in their advanced years, cope with members and

Jocelyn Galsworthy

the general public who are not always as courteous as they might be. In general, club administrators all over the country are sympathetic to the artist and I am usually overwhelmed by the kindness and tolerance I have encountered. I have stretched everyone's patience at times, especially when I am painting until dusk and get locked into the ground. (This has happened on more than one occasion.)

I have been very lucky with radio and television coverage since painting my first Test Match in 1994. I first met Henry Blofeld at Pauline Johnston's Lord's Test Party in 1995 and he offered to give me a mention on Test Match Special. 'Remind me', he said. I did, and he has never failed. On my return from Australia, I received a postcard from a cricket-mad friend saying 'my radio tells me you are on the other side of the world'. Peter Baxter, the Test Match Special producer, is equally good. We always seem to meet, particularly abroad, on the days before a match when I am struggling to complete the background and Peter is wrapped in yards of cable, trying to sort out the problems to keep the show on the air.

Television has given my career a great boost, and I have had generous support from both the BBC and Sky Sports. The commentators, David Gower, Mark Nicholas and Richie Benaud, have always made genuinely complimentary remarks about my work. In 1993 Christopher Martin-Jenkins bought my painting of cricket at Radley College, where both his sons were in the XI during their school lives. It pleased me greatly to sell a cricket painting to one of our most prominent cricket writers and broadcasters. At Trent Bridge in 1995, the BBC focused on my painting at intervals throughout the Test Match. This happened again at Trent Bridge in 1998 and the response from the general public was gratifying. I like to think that people are genuinely intrigued by the idea that the match they are watching is being painted, and that they will have the opportunity to buy, if not the original, then perhaps a print of the occasion. I make many unknown friends each time they catch a glimpse of me on screen and I can testify at first hand to the power of television which, in my case, has been of enormous benefit. TWI, filming for Sky Sports in the West Indies, gave me constant attention and came round with the mobile unit whenever an opportunity arose. I have found the media quietly amazed to see me turning up in foreign parts, and managing to secure prime positions without any official backing. In Australia, John Gayleard, producer for Sky Sports, was always receptive when told of my presence and quite amused when I unerringly found his lorry to give him my location.

At Taunton, during the 1999 World Cup, I went in search of Paul Davies, one of the BBC producers. The production team invited me into their lorry to view the mass of screens from which the producer controls the coverage. I admire the engineers who handle yards and yards of cable, in all weathers, to make transmission possible, and then pack it all up on a sad and empty ground, drive miles and miles to the next venue and start all over again. The cameramen, too, have amazing stamina and withstand the elements in a remarkable way. They are either roasting or freezing cold, and must stand in one position for hours on end – quite a thought when we are watching from our comfortable armchairs.

Being accepted and recognised by the cricket fraternity has been a long, hard struggle. Although women's cricket has a higher profile than before and women are often in control of various aspects of administration such as marketing, it is still a man's world.

For the future, I would like to paint cricket grounds in various parts of the world, including some areas of Europe where the game is played to an increasingly high standard every year. There is also a wealth of beautiful and interesting British cricket grounds still waiting to be painted. Portraiture of cricketers is another area which I would like to explore. I sometimes think back to the early days in my career as a cricket artist, to all the effort, determination and sheer hard work which have gone into producing paintings of which I am proud. I am never happier than when I am with the cricket fraternity, painting this intelligent game. In my opinion, it still upholds the highest standards of fair play, and still has a great influence on a youngster's character.

As an artist travelling the length and breadth of England, following our team when they play abroad, I continually meet distinguished cricket writers and broadcasters. In our different ways, we are all passionate about this most English of games, and we all pray for its renaissance in this country. In the meantime, I shall continue to paint cricket, whenever and wherever I can, and it will be my greatest joy one day to be at my easel when our English side reclaims the Ashes.

Willow Warblers v Hurlingham Club, 1999
I designed the colours for the Willow Warblers, run by Tom & Mike Bristowe.

pastel

The Royal Artillery Ground at Woolwich   *pastel*

Jocelyn Galsworthy

County Ground, Worcester

pastel

The Royal Green Jackets v Gemini at St Cross, Winchester   *pastel*

Surrey v Middlesex, The Oval

pastel

The MCC at Arundel

pastel

Broadhalfpenny Down near Hambledon

pastel

Hurstbourne Priors, Hampshire

pastel

Index

Page numbers in *italics* refer to an illustration.